IMAGES
of America

IBM IN
ENDICOTT

Christmas 2020
Michael Sackeim

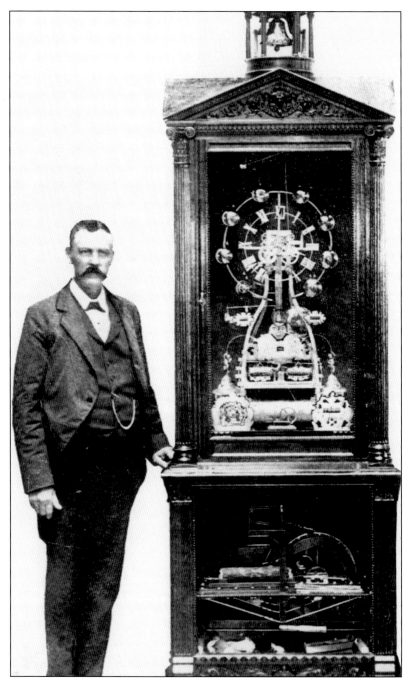

Willard Bundy's spectacular eight-foot-tall clock was exhibited at the 1876 Philadelphia centennial. The workings were all visible, and most of the 3,100 pieces were plated with silver or gold. The clock was the only one of its kind in the world—a totally original creation by Bundy, not a copy of someone else's design. This clock exemplifies the creative mechanical genius of Willard L. Bundy, who was responsible for one of the building blocks of the great International Business Machines Company: time recording machines. The clock was a marvel of craftsmanship from the master clockmaker and jeweler.

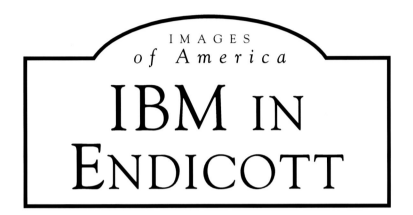

IMAGES of America
IBM IN ENDICOTT

Ed Aswad and Suzanne M. Meredith

Copyright © 2005 by Ed Aswad and Suzanne M. Meredith
ISBN 978-0-7385-3700-9

Published by Arcadia Publishing
Charleston, South Carolina

Printed in the United States of America

Library of Congress Catalog Card Number: 2004110969

For all general information contact Arcadia Publishing at:
Telephone 843-853-2070
Fax 843-853-0044
E-mail sales@arcadiapublishing.com
For customer service and orders:
Toll-Free 1-888-313-2665

Visit us on the Internet at www.arcadiapublishing.com

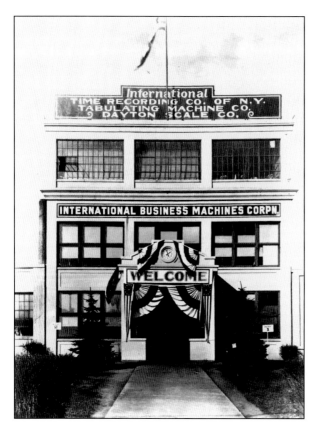

At Endicott's Flag Day celebration in 1929, the signs on the IBM building still reflected the names of three of the companies that had combined to form the International Business Machines Corporation.

Contents

Foreword   6

Introduction   7

Timeline   8

1. Bundy of Binghamton   9

2. From Bottom Land to Boomtown   23

3. IBM and the War Years   95

4. Tent City   105

5. IBM Serves Earth and Space   115

Acknowledgments   128

Bibliography   128

Foreword

In 1906, the International Time Recording Company, having outgrown its facility in Binghamton, moved its operations to Endicott, New York. This move planted the seed for a long relationship between the Greater Endicott area and a company that would eventually become IBM.

Growing up just outside of Endicott in the 1970s and 1980s, the son of an "IBMer," I had difficulty distinguishing between the community and the company. I attended preschool on IBM's Homestead property at the Children's Club, spent summers swimming and playing sports at the IBM Country Club, and thought that everyone had a parent who was an engineer, scientist, or computer programmer.

There were yearly family days with amusement park rides, games, and an abundance of food. If one of my teams was lucky enough to win a trophy we celebrated at a massive banquet, always attended by famous sports figures, completing the somewhat idealistic and surreal experience that was real life in IBM Valley.

Thomas J. Watson Sr., IBM's chief executive for nearly 40 years, believed strongly in developing employee loyalty. Therefore, the company pioneered the offering of group insurance coverage, survivor benefits, and paid vacations. This led to tremendous financial success for the company, and set the stage for my life in some of the truly golden years of IBM in Broome County. Many of the philosophies and practices implemented by IBM's earliest management made these experiences possible.

The seemingly constant turnover of students in my school was just part of living in a town dominated by the company we called "I've Been Moved." My personal decision to become an engineer was strongly influenced by my formative years as an IBM kid in an IBM town. In those days, being an IBMer was a way of life defined by the unique relationship between the company and the community. Any worker was envied and considered to have reached a pinnacle on the employment ladder when employed by IBM: the job was practically guaranteed for life.

The collection of images in this volume will take you back in time, on a journey into the history of one of America's greatest corporations and the community that it helped to create.

—Brian Meredith

Introduction

Mankind was created with a need to mark his passage through time—to record the moments of sunlight, the ocean tides, the span of life. Computing the seasonal changes and the weight of grains became a necessity as civilization evolved. For centuries, tools for calculation were of simple design: an abacus, a sundial, scales, and stones. Even the great monolithic Stonehenge of England may have been a device for gauging astronomical data.

IBM is heir to all the ideas for innovative ciphering machines of the past. The company used basic principles of data processing to bring the world into the age of the computer.

Progress from granite blocks and beads to punched data cards to computer chips as small as raindrops—all are the historical roots of the great corporate legend International Business Machines. The company began with a small firm of visionaries whose first factory was a dismal garret—Bundy of Binghamton—where computing technology was born. But Bundy Manufacturing was just one component; in all, 13 original companies combined to form the foundation of IBM.

Endicott, New York, played a pivotal role in the international profile of computer technology. The phenomenal growth of the village and its symbiotic relationship with the computer giant are portrayed in photographs and succinct captions.

Not all events, people, images, or products of the industry could be included in this volume. The scope has been limited to the early days of IBM in Broome County and the changes wrought by its dominant presence. Pictured are just a few of the notable moments during the golden years of "Big Blue" in the Valley of Opportunity.

Timeline

1896—Dr. Herman Hollerith founds the Tabulating Machine Company with his patented data-storing and computing machines. Machines are used in the 1890 U.S. census.
1891—The Computing Scale Company is formed by Edward Canby and Orange O. Ozais, of Dayton, Ohio, by purchasing the scale patent from Julius E. Pitrat.
1889—Willard and Harlow Bundy and A. Ward Ford organize the Bundy Manufacturing Company to produce mechanical time recorders in Binghamton, New York.
1900—The International Time Recording Company (ITR) forms as a holding company for a conglomerate of Bundy Manufacturing and several other businesses.
1906—Endicott, New York, is chosen as the site for construction of a new ITR plant.
1907—The Dey Time Recording Company is brought under the ITR umbrella.
1911—Banker Charles Flint organizes the merger of companies; all are incorporated in New York State as the Computing-Tabulating-Recording Company (CTR).
1914—Thomas J. Watson joins CTR as general manager.
1915—Thomas J. Watson becomes president.
1919—CTR enters the European business market amid great demand for its products.
1923—CTR offices open in Latin America and the Far East.
1924—CTR becomes the International Business Machines Company (IBM).
1926—IBM wins recognition for its product line at the Sesquicentennial Exposition in Philadelphia. The total number of employees reaches 3,953.
1929—The stock market crashes, but IBM manages to grow and prosper, adding more employees and paying a stock dividend of 5 percent.
1933—A new education and engineering building is constructed in Endicott; Electromatic Typewriters is purchased by IBM.
1934—The Dayton Scale Division is sold.
1936—IBM wins the U.S. Social Security contract.
1938—T. J. Watson Sr. earns the second-highest salary in the country, at $453,000.
1941–1945—All IBM facilities are offered to the government for the war effort.
1949—The World Trade Corporation is formed as a subsidiary to handle all overseas operations.
1950—IBM offers all facilities to the government for Korean War work.
1952—Thomas J. Watson Jr. is installed as IBM president.
1957—The gross income of IBM reaches $1 billion.
1958—The International Time Recording Division is sold to Simplex Corporation.
1961—IBM employs more than 116,000 workers.
1964—The most important product to date in the corporation's history is announced: the IBM System/360 concept in computers.
1968—The Apollo space program receives important technical support from IBM.
1994—IBM Owego is sold to the Loral Corporation.
1996—The Loral Corporation merges with Martin Marietta.
2004—All IBM facilities in the Southern Tier have been sold.

One
BUNDY OF BINGHAMTON

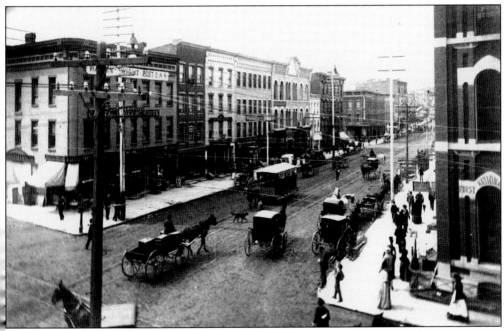

Court Street was the main thoroughfare in downtown Binghamton when the Bundy Time Recorder Company began looking for quarters where a revolutionary new product could be developed. Binghamton was a growing and vibrant city with a population of approximately 34,000, dirt roads, and a horse-drawn trolley. The first location for Bundy was in the back corner of a small loft in Franey's old gristmill, located at 40 Commercial Alley, not far from the scene above. Entrepreneurs who worked on the narrow street referred to the location as "Mud Alley." This photograph was taken in the late 1890s.

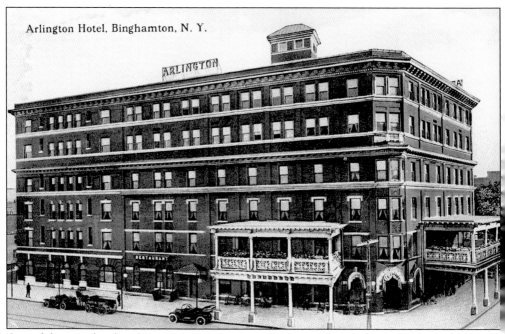

One of the grandest hotels to operate in Broome County opened for business in 1888 near the Binghamton railroad station: the Arlington. Willard Bundy had invented a time-recording device but needed financial backing to produce the invention. In 1889, in an Arlington parlor, amidst gracious furnishings and the exceptional art collection of hotel proprietor Edward M. Tierney, Willard and his brother Harlow Bundy met with W. Ford and his son A. Ward Ford to organize the Bundy Manufacturing Company, the first time-recording company in the world. These photographs show the stately exterior and interior of the old Arlington. The building was demolished in 1967 during a bout of urban renewal zeal. The site remains a barren asphalt lot.

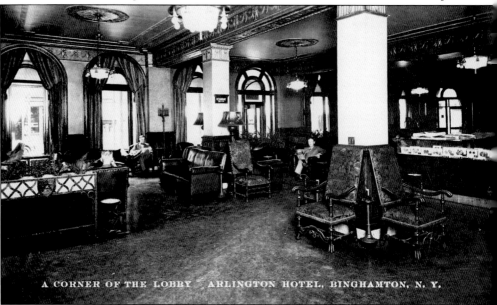

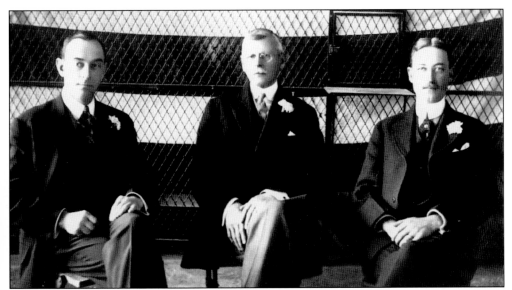

Willard Bundy of Auburn, New York, was a jeweler and inventive genius in the early 1880s. He devised a time recorder for use in the workplace. Each employee was assigned a key with a number on it. When the key was inserted in the recorder and turned, the number of the key and the time were printed on paper tape. The Bundy Manufacturing Company began with just eight employees and $150,000 capital. The men pictured above were part of the core management of the operation. Willard Bundy (center), superintendent of the company, continued to invent many specialties for corporate production. His brother Harlow (left), an attorney, saw the commercial viability of the time clock and had the entrepreneurial expertise to manage and promote the product. A. Ward Ford (right) and his father invested heavily in the new business. By 1919, the time clocks were in demand by businesses throughout the country and were in rapid production at the Endicott plant. The photograph below shows the assembly of time clocks in 1918.

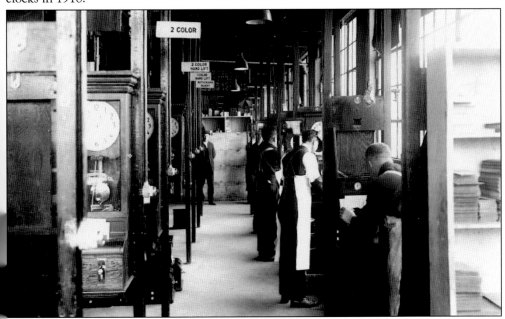

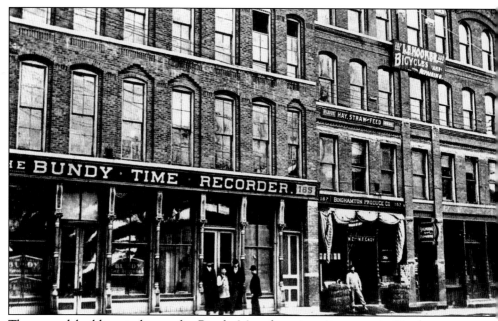

The second building to house the Bundy Manufacturing Company in Binghamton was o Water Street. By 1898, nearly 9,000 Bundy time recorders were on the market. The compan promoted the devices as being guaranteed to solve "vexatious questions of recording employe time." The federal government adopted the machines for use in post offices, saving th government millions of dollars. This building later housed the Link Piano Company, wher Edwin A. Link developed a pilot-training machine that changed the future of aviation.

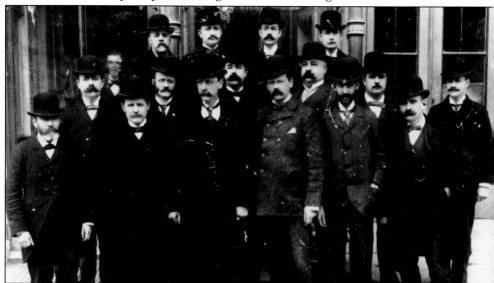

Members of the Bundy Manufacturing sales force are already dressed in the "uniform of success as they meet in front of the Binghamton building in 1899. When Thomas J. Watson acquire the company, he often told employees that "clothes go a long way toward making a businessma a gentleman." The white shirt, tie, and dark suit continued to be the marks of appropriate attir for IBM employees for many decades. Watson also insisted on formality of speech, whereby a but the closest friend was addressed with the title "Mr."

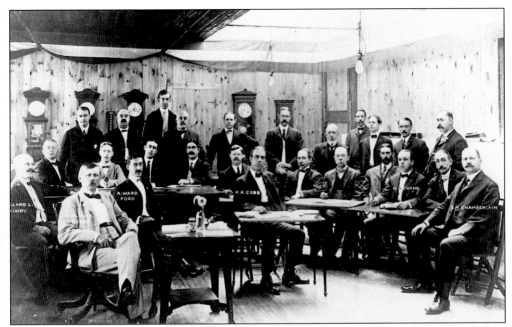

The pioneers of timekeeping are pictured in 1899. The gentlemen whose names are imprinted on the photograph are often referred to as the "Big Six" of the time recorder organization. George Green, once mayor of Binghamton, served as president, and J. P. Fiebig was vice president. A guiding strategy for the company was that the pioneering spirit of discovery should never cease.

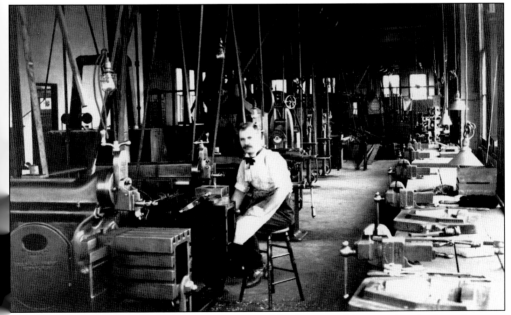

T. J. Watson demanded perfection in every area of the factories. No scratches in the paint were allowed—particularly on the machines he had painted green. Walls and other equipment were also tinted "Watson Green," because after some research he was convinced that the shade of green was soothing to workers and easier on the eyes. Above is a 1919 view of a factory.

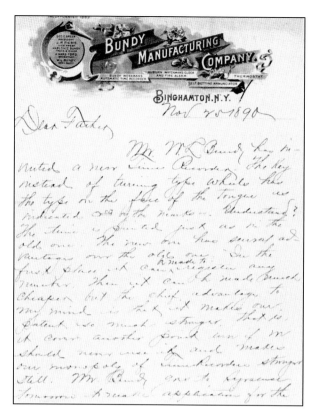

The 1891 minutes of the Bundy Manufacturing Company stated that for three weeks in a row a resolution was passed to "borrow $250. each of Mr. G. Green, J. P. Fiebig, Wm. L. Ford & H. E. Bundy." The funds were needed to keep the company functioning until profits could be realized. The letter at left, written by A. Ward Ford to his father, indicates that Willard Bundy was continuing to invent improvements to the time recorders.

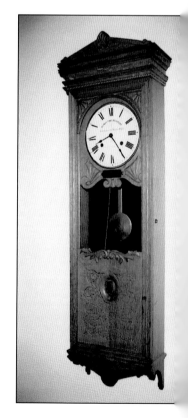

An early Bundy clock was promoted to customers with the following slogans: "Your time clock is your purse. Are the strings drawn taut?" "Time is your chief stock in trade." "There is great wealth in carefully managed hours." "When we are wasting time we are wasting lives." "Place value on every minute with our machines."

In this letter, of which only the second page has survived, A. Ward Ford asks his father to intervene with one of the other founders of the company, Mr. Evans. A plan of action was needed to see that the Bundy Company progressed in the field of time accounting and recording. The letterhead has been slightly altered from that previously used.

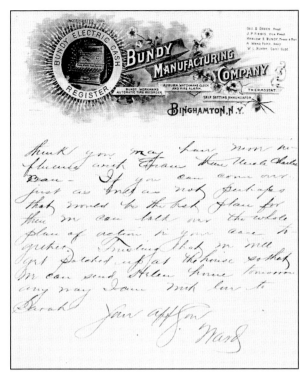

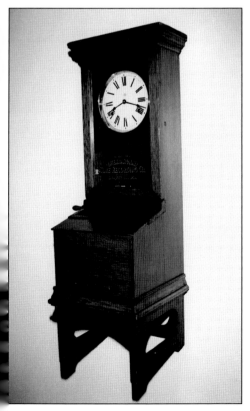

Clocks manufactured by the International Time Recording Company (ITR) and the Computing-Tabulating-Recording Company (CTR) were sold through the following advertising: "Time lost is time gone forever." "Men use minutes to make money." "We [ITR] are in service to time." "The use of CTR machines makes more time available for creative work." "Conserve that most precious of all commodities, TIME!" "Excellence over time." "Time becomes more valuable to business every day . . . don't lose time . . . use our machines to keep time your servant."

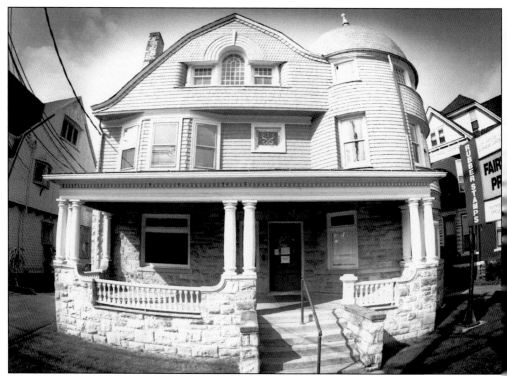

Harlow Bundy and his family lived on Main Street in Binghamton in this 1880s Queen Ann–style home. The preserved building now houses a commercial enterprise and the Bundy Museum and Galleries. These photographs show the exterior as it is today and the interior of the dining room in 1901.

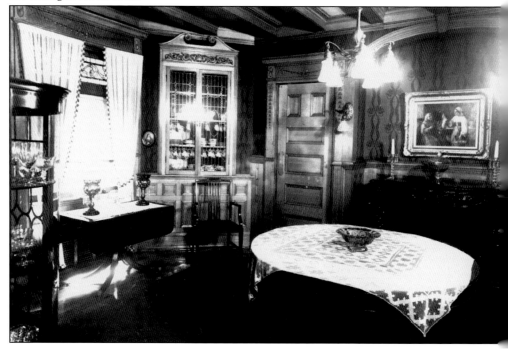

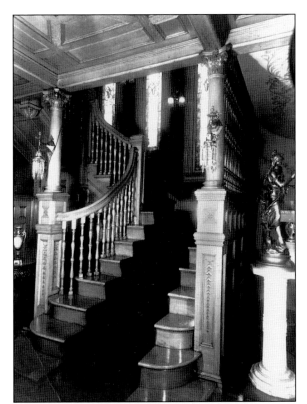

The grand entry staircase and the Bundy parlor are shown in these 1901 photographs. The elaborate woodwork and fireplace remain intact. Conservation efforts are in progress today. The wallpaper will be authentically reproduced, and the architecturally significant interior will be appointed with period antiques and exhibits.

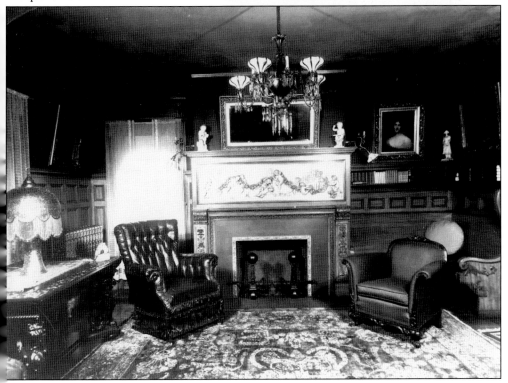

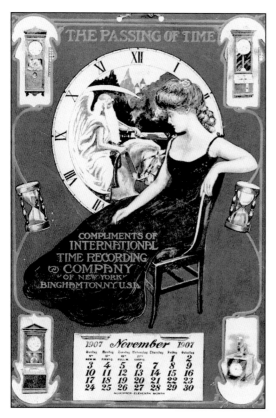

A 1907 calendar promoting the International Time Recording Company of Binghamton reflects an art nouveau style popular in the era. The ITR motto at this time was "Safeguarding the Minute." Many devices were produced to help businesses conserve minutes and accurately record time spent by employees, including card and dial recorders, and autograph and key machines. The company stated, "Our machines make every man the master of his own timekeeping."

Information for customers and employees was provided in the magazine *Time*. This issue was printed in 1907, and thousands of copies were mailed across the country. In 1935, the publication was changed to *Think*, featuring articles on recent inventions, education, art, and company news. By 1946, IBM's *Think* magazine was being distributed to 80,000 people, including leaders in government, business, the arts, and education, as well as all employees. Another publication for employees, the *ITR Factory Record*, was first printed in 1918.

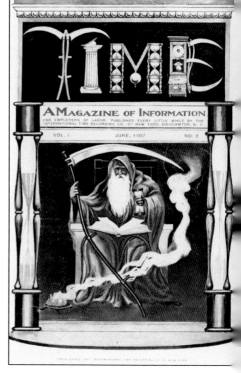

Dr. Herman Hollerith was a statistician employed by the federal government. In 1886 he tested his invention of a mechanical tabulating system to record vital statistics for the Baltimore Department of Health. In 1889 Hollerith received a patent for the tabulating machine. The device used a process that reduced facts to a usable form by recording the data as a defined pattern of holes punched in a card. The inspiration for the invention came from three sources: the Jacquard loom, player-piano rolls, and the punched holes in railway tickets. When the U.S. census bureau sponsored a contest to find an efficient means of tabulating the next census, Hollerith won the competition. He used his invention successfully in computing the 1890 and 1900 censuses. By 1896, Hollerith had organized the Tabulating Machine Company in Washington, D.C., the world's first electric tabulating and accounting machine enterprise. Pictured are a youthful Hollerith and the details of his counting machine.

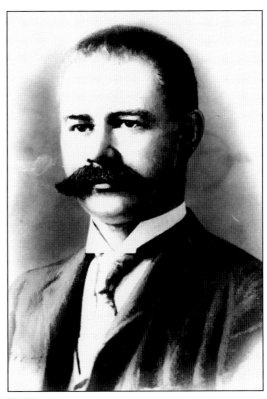

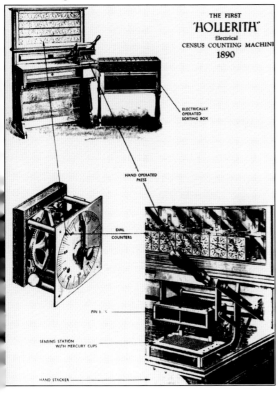

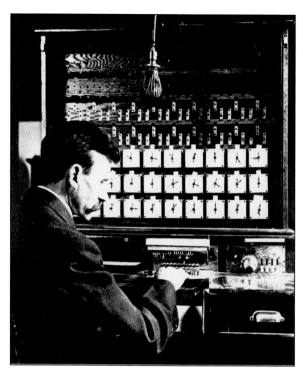

The Hollerith Circuit-Closing Press appears here in 1890. Although Hollerith took out new patents nearly every year when initial development of the system was in progress, he did not want his name on the machines. After his business was sold to the Computing-Tabulating-Recording Company (CTR), Hollerith remained associated with the company as a consulting engineer. He continued to be feisty and independent, and was not particularly impressed with Thomas Watson. Born in 1860, Herman Hollerith died in 1929.

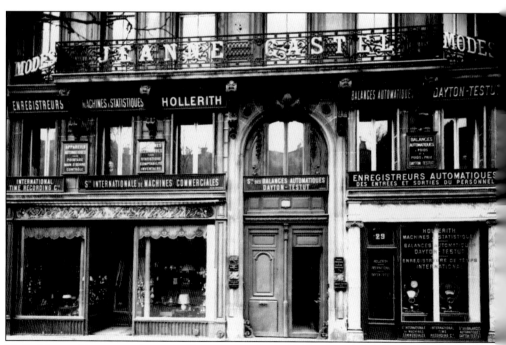

Hollerith machines were in use in Europe as early as 1910, planting the seed for the future of foreign trade in the IBM Company. Headquarters for foreign sales was this building in Paris, France, seen c.1920.

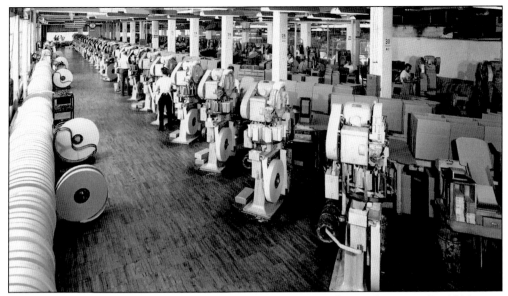

The Industrial Revolution inspired progress in every area of manufacturing. In 1916, in a small loft on Sixth Avenue in New York City, a laboratory was established for CTR. There, Frank Carroll worked to design a printer that was faster than the popular Powers machine. Mass production of punched cards at a high rate of speed was the goal. He invented a printing cylinder that revolutionized the manufacture of tabulating cards, eventually producing 850 cards per minute. The Carroll rotary card presses are pictured above in 1923.

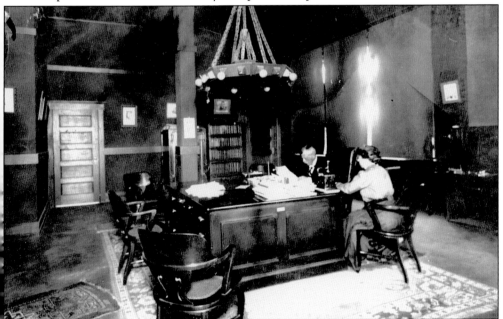

Harlow E. Bundy was a successful attorney when he became one of the founders of the Bundy Manufacturing Company. This photograph was taken in his Endicott office in 1911, the year the Computing-Tabulating-Recording Company (CTR) was formed by joining the Computing Scale Company with the International Time Recording Company (ITR). It was also the year that Hollerith lost the 1910 census contract and sold his business to CTR.

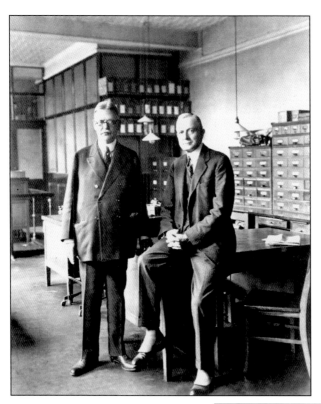

George W. Fairchild, of Oneonta, New York, became one of the most ardent supporters of the Endicott complex of the International Time Recording Company. In 1896, he became an active part of the management and took $5,000 in capital stock. Fairchild formed ITR as the selling agency for the Bundy Manufacturing Corporation, serving as its president for several years. He was also a United States congressman. Upon Fairchild's death in 1924, T. J. Watson became the chief executive officer. Fairchild (left) and Watson pose in 1920.

George E. Green, born in 1858 in Kirkwood, New York, gained prominence as mayor of Binghamton, state senator, and state commissioner of excise for New York. An early investor in the Bundy Company, Green was eventually elected president of the International Time Recording Company. His extensive experience as a politician eased the way for the new corporation. At the time of his death in 1917, Green was widely known as an honest and influential force in the community.

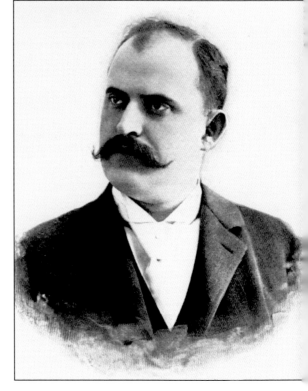

Two
FROM BOTTOM LAND TO BOOMTOWN

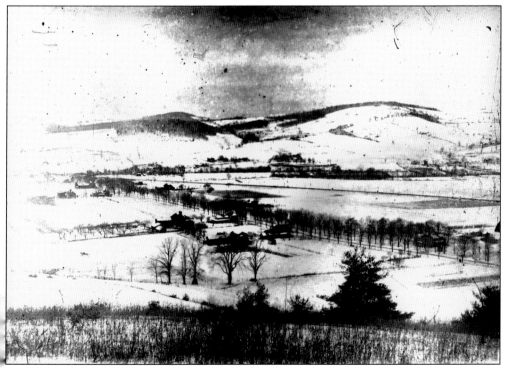

In 1907, just seven years after the founding of Endicott by the great shoe-manufacturing concern Endicott-Johnson (EJ), Bundy of Binghamton moved to the new village. Endicott was often called "the Magic City" because it rose so quickly from farmland fields and swamps to a bustling commercial center. This photograph shows the valley as it was prior to the construction of factories and streets.

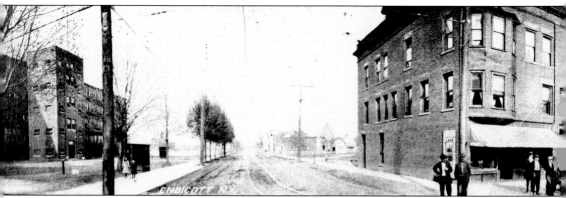

Endicott streets were configured so the main commercial area on Washington Avenue intersected with North Street, the prime industrial section. The city was planned as an employee paradise, with everything necessary for the comfort of workers within walking

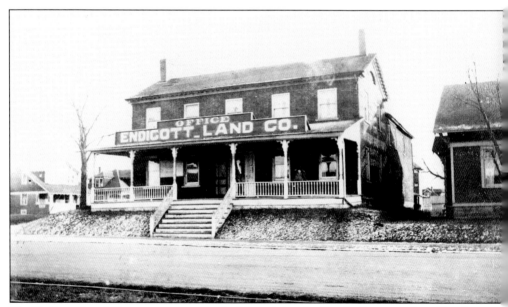

The Endicott Land Company was credited with enticing the Bundy Company from Binghamton to Endicott when the manufacturer had a need for larger quarters. Cheap land, abundant water, rail transportation, and a labor pool were exactly what Bundy required. Owners of the largest employer in Broome County, Endicott-Johnson, encouraged the timekeepers to move to what they promised would grow into a "blue ribbon city." The land company headquarters (pictured) were in a historic home once owned by an early settler in the town of Union.

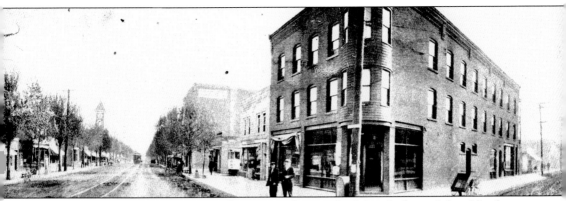

distance. This early-1900s image shows the crossroads—on the left side (page 24) is North Street, and on the right (above) is Washington Avenue, with its horse-drawn trolleys, dirt thoroughfares, and wooden sidewalks.

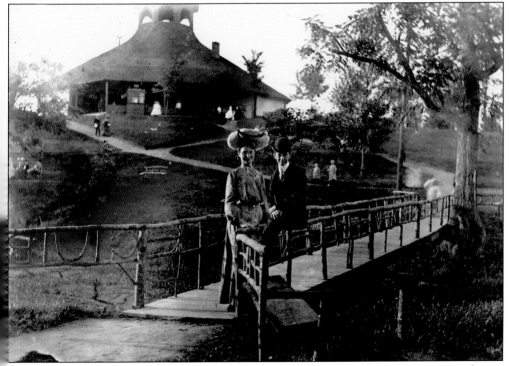

The congenial community atmosphere and suitable resources for leisure recreation were factors in persuading the Bundy Company to move to Endicott. Casino Park was located along the Susquehanna River at the south end of Washington Avenue. Excursions from all over the county converged at the park to take advantage of the racetrack, elaborate gardens, picnic facilities, sporting events, first-rate entertainment, and dancing in the park clubhouse.

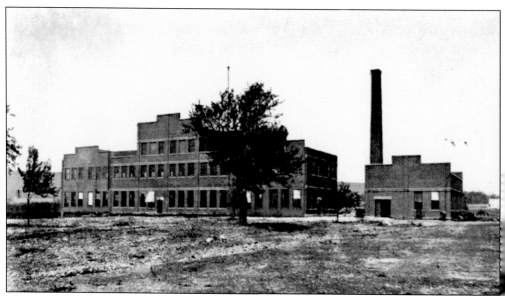

The Bundy Adding Machine Company constructed a special power plant near its new factory, complete with up-to-date Ingersol engines. Massive engines like the one pictured below were used to operate and heat the entire facility. The factory building was of the most modern design, constructed entirely of concrete. The power plant was located to the right of the factory for safety purposes, as shown above.

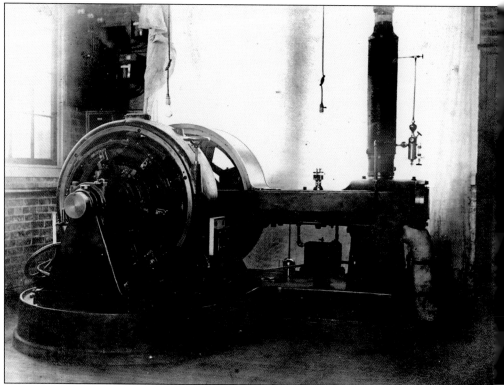

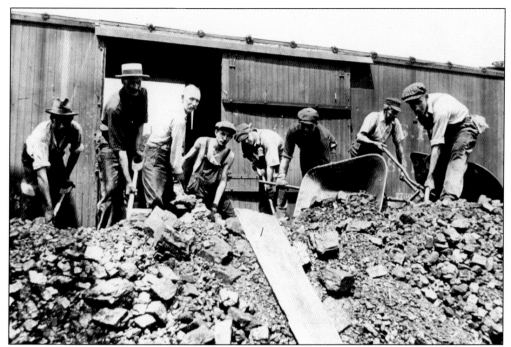

By the 1920s, CTR had begun heating its buildings with coal transported from the nearby railroad siding. The labor-intensive process was all completed with manpower and wheelbarrows. Pictured are employees unloading the rail cars and moving tons of number nine coal.

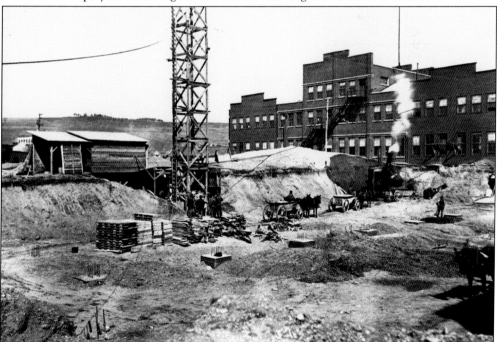

Another new building was constructed for the Endicott timekeepers in 1920. The corporation employed more than 3,000 people, and its earnings had tripled since 1914. Business was calculated to be up more than 50 percent over the previous year.

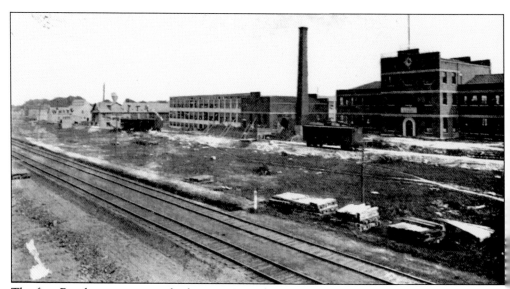

The first Bundy structure was built in 1907, and in 1911, a new addition was constructed on the ITR campus at a cost of $100,000. The new structure was completely fireproof with a steel frame. ITR built along the rail lines as it planned for future growth. The iron horse connected Endicott facilities with markets around the country. All distant points were made commercial neighbors by the railroads. But in 1922, the rail companies were in serious financial difficulty. CTR set a goal to save the railroads money and gain themselves customers. "There are too many clerks. . . . Put more of our machines to work" was the timekeeper's advice. ITR was becoming known for the excellence of its products turned out by "trained minds and skilled artisans." These photographs show the progressive growth of IBM and the surrounding areas and the prominent rail lines. Above is a view from the 1920s, and below is an image from the 1940s.

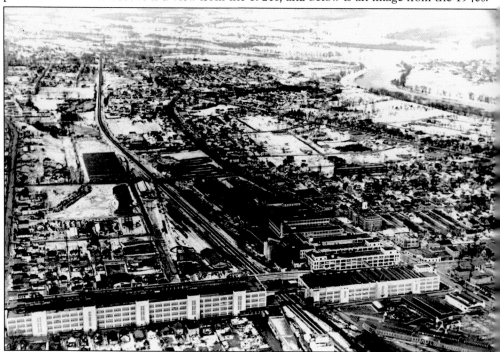

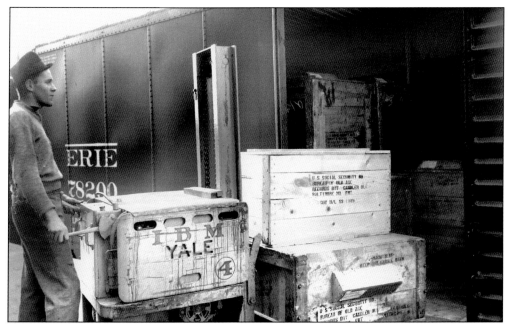

When the United States passed the Social Security Act in 1935, IBM made a successful bid for the accounting process. It was the world's biggest bookkeeping job. IBM handled the details with the "accrual card that tells the story of your laboring life using electronic eyes and pine needle fingers." It was hailed as a task that would have been impossible without the $150,000 of electronic machines that "do everything but take their hats off and bow." According to a *Binghamton Press* report, the boxes being loaded on the train are destined for the Social Security Department.

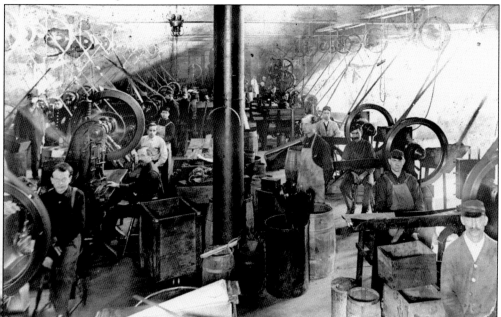

One of the earliest photographs of the ITR punch press department displays how some of the thousands of parts for time recorders and tabulating machines were fabricated. The parts were made from cold-rolled steel and brass, then blanked and formed into all kinds of shapes.

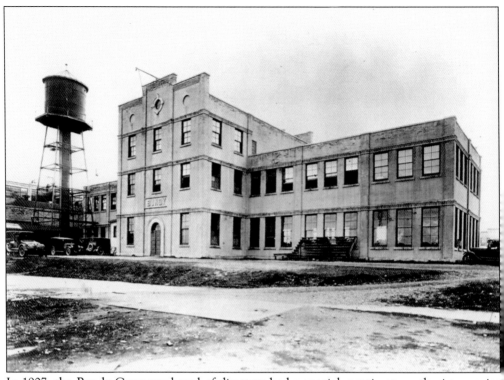

In 1907, the Bundy Company board of directors had a special meeting to authorize a major expenditure for the construction of a 25,000-gallon water tank at the Endicott site (above). By 1916, this structure was showing its age, and one night the tank completely collapsed, as shown below.

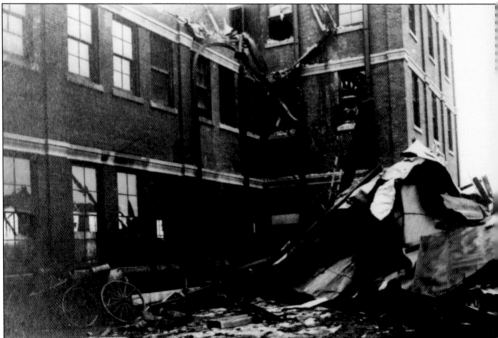

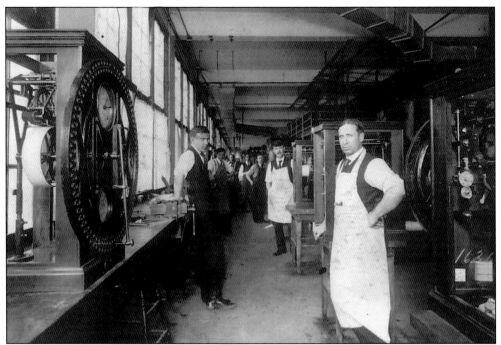

In 1888, Dr. Alexander Dey, a Scottish physician, patented the Dey Dial Time Recorder. The machine held employee numbers around the circumference of a large ring, and was constructed in three sizes—for 50, 100, and 150 employees. In 1907, ITR acquired the Dey Time Recording Company and, in 1908, moved it to Endicott. A massive effort was made to relocate the machinery and everything involved without ceasing the labors of making the time registers. "Equipment was moved at night from its location in the 'Salt City' of Syracuse, set up the next morning in Endicott and in working order by the next day," reported the *Binghamton Press*. Employees arriving in Endicott were temporarily housed at the Matoon Hotel. The photograph above shows the final factory assembly of dial recorders in the 1920s. The image below shows the time recorder in use at a business in 1926.

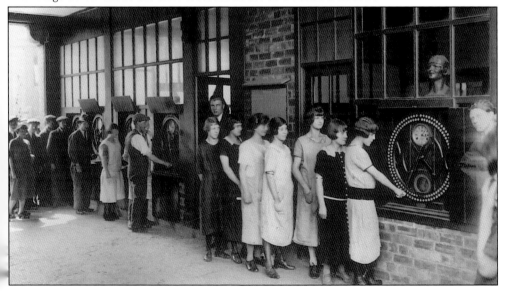

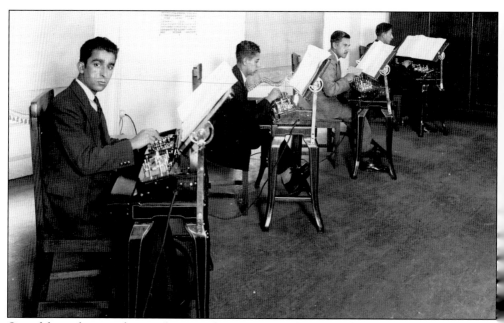

One of the earliest purchasers of statistical computing machines was the government of Chile. The first use was to compile information for the state rail system. An early nickname for the mechanism was the "Hollerith Statistical Piano." The scene above almost resembles a piano orchestra.

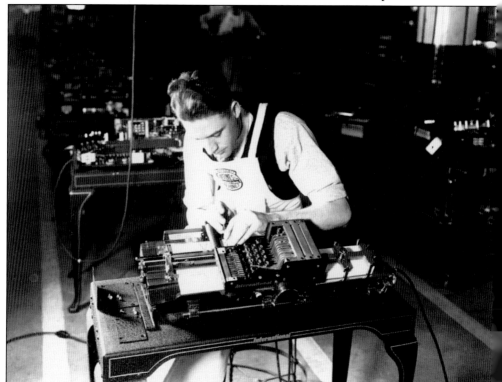

Skilled mechanics were trained to keep the modern compiling devices in prime working order. A key-punch machine is adjusted in 1930 in the above photograph.

Pictured is the vertical tabulating card sorter in 1908. The design changed very little over the next 20 years.

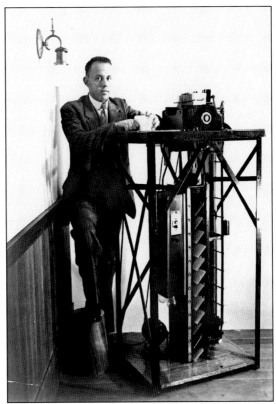

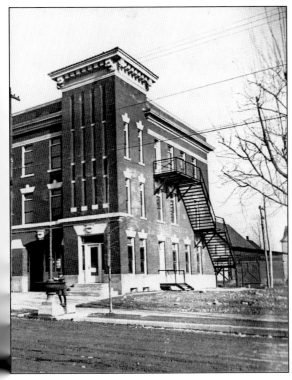

In 1911, when the time-recording business was new in Endicott, one of the public facilities was a communal water fountain (at lower left of photograph) on Washington Avenue that was equipped with a single tin cup for dipping. Workers agitated for a bubbling-type water dispenser because hundreds of people drank from the cup daily and it could sometimes be found in the middle of the street or under the sidewalk. Feet and hands were washed in the water, and pets drank from the same dipper as humans. This was life for ITR clockmakers in the "good old days."

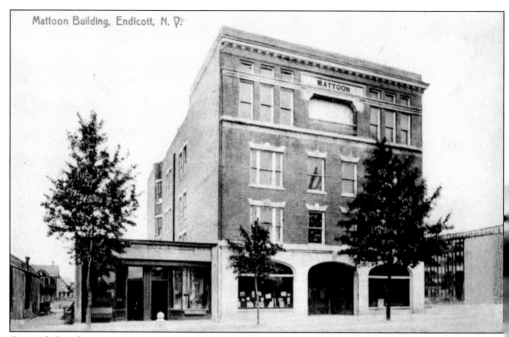

One of the first structures built on Washington Avenue was the Matoon Hotel (pictured above), a social center and temporary home for new employees. In 1911, the clockmakers of ITR gained a reputation as royal entertainers. A dance held at the Matoon in the large hall on the fourth floor was crowded until a late hour, with rooms attractively decorated, and music provided by a full-piece orchestra. People from all over the valley attended to socialize with the clockmaker crew. In 1915, the hotel also housed the Endicott Free Library. The ITR staff was instrumental in the library's formation and donated a high-grade self-winding Master clock that had works made by the famous Seth Thomas Clock Company. The clock was placed in a prominent position near the librarian's desk. The photograph below shows the ITR clockmakers at a dance held in the Bundy Building in 1918. Only a small sum was charged of persons who attended with lady friends and a much smaller sum for ladies who attended without escorts.

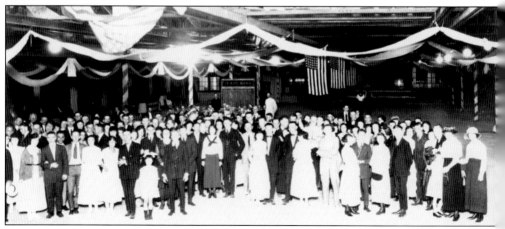

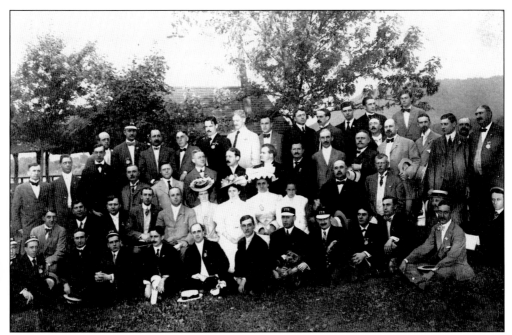

The family atmosphere among "timekeepers" was furthered by a clambake at Endicott's Casino Park in 1907. Gentlemen in the front row are wearing ITR ball caps. Noticeable in the picture is Harlow Bundy, the last man on the right in the second row (kneeling).

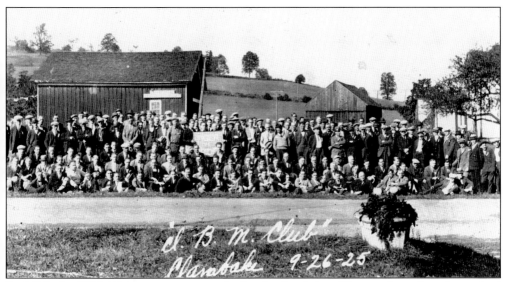

By 1925, the IBM Club was sponsoring the family clambakes. The number of employees had increased to 3,698, but the workers remained a close group, socializing and participating in company sports teams after hours.

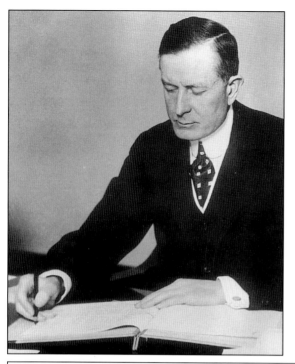

Thomas J. Watson Sr., a famous industrial leader of the 20th century, is the man who is most associated with creating IBM. At the age of 40, in 1914, Watson joined the Computing-Tabulating-Recording Company (CTR) as general manager. By 1915, he was president of the 400-employee concern. He invested his own capital in CTR and reinvested corporate funds into development. In 1924, the company's name was changed to International Business Machines (IBM). During lunch at the Waldorf Astoria Hotel in New York City in 1936, Watson accepted for IBM the first prize in the Industrial Modernization Contest sponsored by *Forbes* magazine. The modern plants and the establishment of employee country clubs set an example for corporations throughout the world.

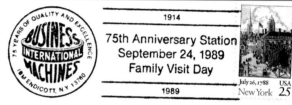

HAIL TO THE I. B. M.

Words by Fred W. Tappe Music by Vittorio Giannini

Lift up our proud and loyal voices,
  Sing out in accents strong and true,
With hearts and hands to you devoted,
  And inspiration ever new;
Your ties of friendship cannot sever,
  Your glory time will never stem,
We will toast a name that lives forever,
  Hail to the I. B. M.

Our voices swell in admiration;
  Of T. J. Watson proudly sing;
He'll ever be our inspiration,
  To him our voices loudly ring;
The I. B. M. will sing the praises,
  Of him who brought us world acclaim,
As the volume of our chorus raises,
  Hail to his honored name.

Long after Thomas J. Watson Sr.'s death in 1956, his image was still synonymous with IBM. As the corporate giant celebrated its 75th anniversary in 1989, Watson's photograph and his slogan, "Think," were used on souvenir postcards and envelopes.

Portraits of Thomas Watson Sr. were hung in IBM executive offices throughout the world, always reminding employees of the strict standards expected each day, both at work and after hours. The Watson-bedecked office of Jack Van Gorden in Endicott is pictured in the 1930s. He began working for the company in 1917.

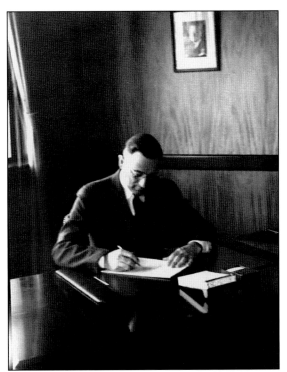

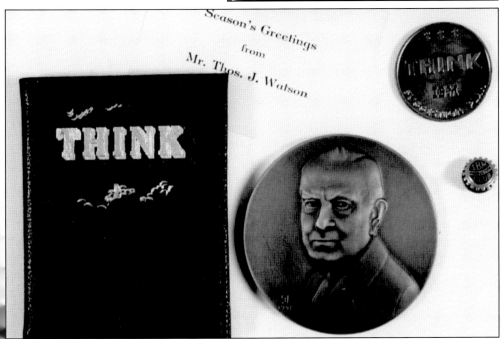

In June 1935, a small leather notebook from IBM, inscribed with "Think" on the cover, was credited with saving the life of a World War II soldier. Carried in a knapsack pocket during a battle in Okinawa, the book diverted a Japanese bullet from the lung area to the shoulder area of PFC Oliver G. Collins. He survived the war and returned to work at IBM. A Think book, medal, token, and IBM Club pin are treasured souvenirs of the golden era of Big Blue in Endicott.

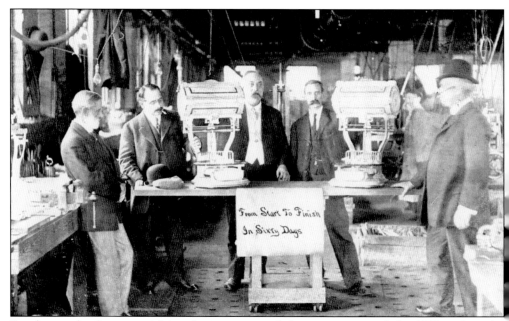

For thousands of years, weighing devices remained the same . . . until the 1890s, when the first computing scale gave the world a new system of weighing and measuring. The Dayton scale changed the needs of every merchant, and the demand grew for the precision instrument that included leveling feet and a free scoop. Dayton scales were guaranteed to meet customers' specifications, and were assembled "from start to finish in sixty days."

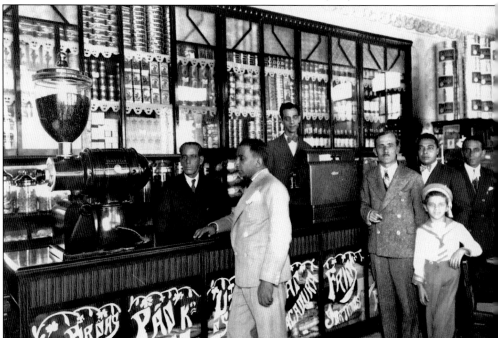

Dayton coffee mills were distributed worldwide, as evidenced by this photograph of a store in South America. Also produced were bacon slicers and meat choppers. In 1934, IBM sold the Dayton Scale Division to the Hobart Manufacturing Company.

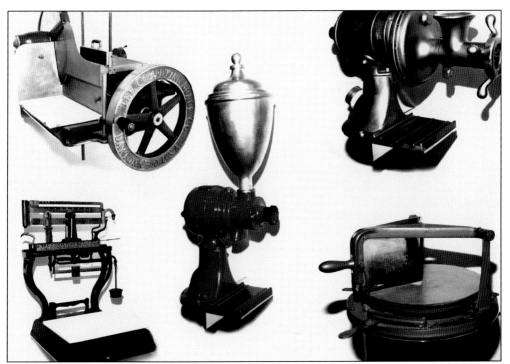

Above is a collage of Dayton equipment. In 1885, Julius E. Pitrap was issued a patent on a new weighing device: the computing scale. Computing the values as it weighed commodities, it was advertised as the most "beautiful and accurate scale in the world," easy to read and of the finest mechanical construction. The coffee mill was billed as a "handsome device that needs cleaning only once a year." And the meat slicer "is guaranteed to attract new trade to your store!" (Photographs by Ed Aswad.)

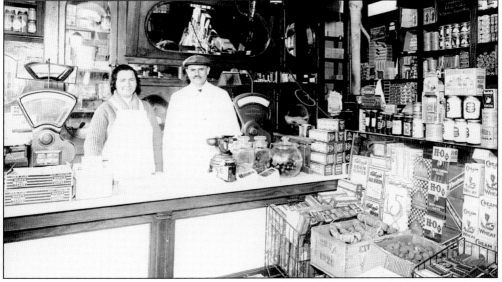

Dayton scales were used at thousands of large and small businesses both nationally and internationally. The photograph shows the scales in use at a mom-and-pop grocery store in New York in the early 1900s.

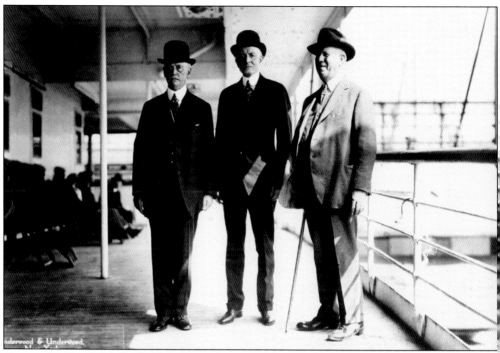

George W. Fairchild (left), T. J. Watson Sr. (center), and Samuel Hastings are pictured in 1919 aboard a ship bound for Europe. The men were working on expanding business into foreign countries.

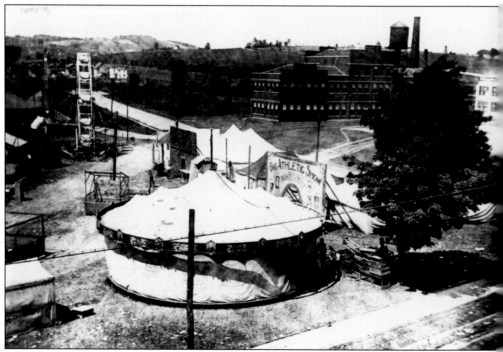

In 1908, traveling circus shows set up big tents on vacant property near the new Endicott ITF buildings, seen in the background.

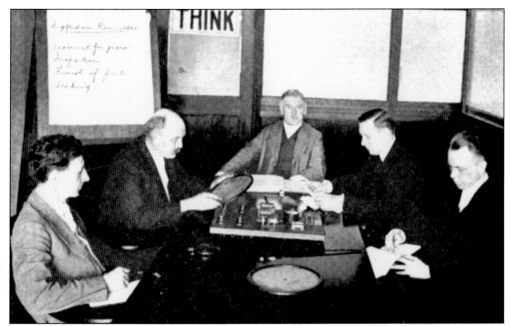

An employee suggestion plan was in place early in the history of IBM. This 1919 photograph shows members of the suggestion committee reviewing some of the ideas submitted. Employees could earn awards for their suggestions. In 1928, most awards were for $1 or $2.50 each. If an idea was outstanding, it might warrant $5. In 1946, a total of $101,824 was awarded for the 9,000 suggestions received during the year. By 1970, the employees of Endicott had been awarded more than $4.5 million through the suggestion plan.

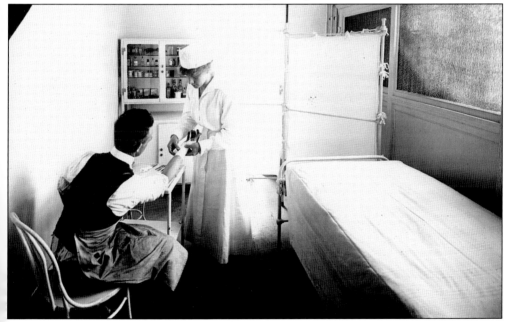

The ITR medical assistance plan for employees was a model of efficiency in 1919. Irene Wagner, the ITR nurse in charge of the plant emergency room, treated more than 3,000 cases in that year. This was considered a good record for a factory of 1,200 employees.

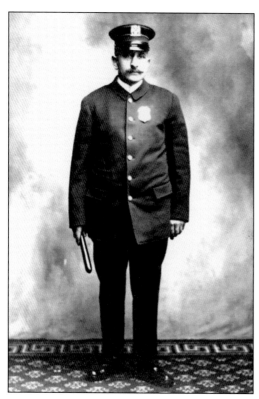

Daniel Frutiger served as chief of police for the village of Endicott from 1913 to 1935, and received a salary of $80 a month. In 1916, the police force comprised a total of three officers, but by 1922, there were eight men guarding the public. The police cooperated with the private-security forces of EJ and IBM to maintain the peace.

The role of IBM's security department was to prevent problems and protect IBM property and employees. Security officers' proficiency was increased by equine and canine assistants.

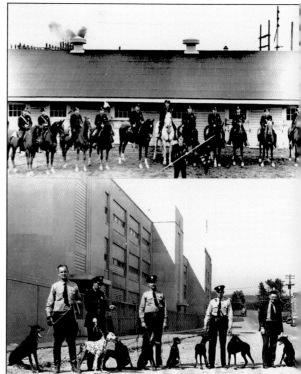

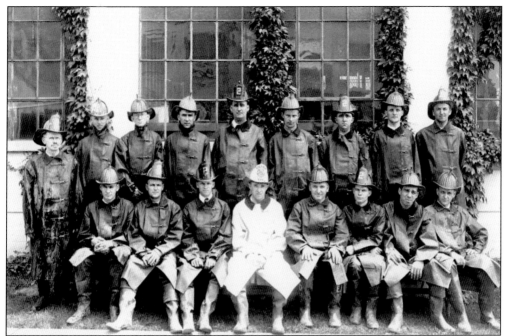

The "Bundy Hooks" were part of the ITR firefighting and fire prevention unit. A 1913 newspaper notice announced the election of company officers at a meeting held in their rooms over the Endicott Lumber and Box Company offices. After the business meeting, a "smoker" was conducted, which included ITR's counterparts in the George F. Johnson fire company. The above photograph of the Bundy Hook and Ladder Company was taken in 1918, and the EJ fire team is pictured in 1926. IBM also produced fire alarm systems for schools and other public buildings. The alarm systems were engineered individually for each client.

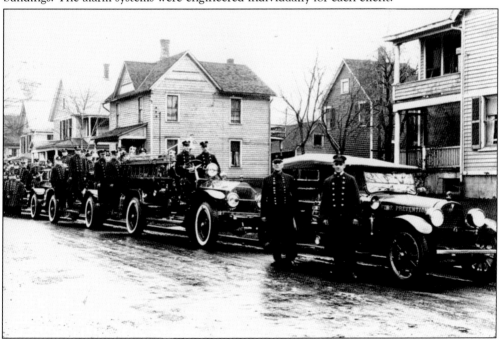

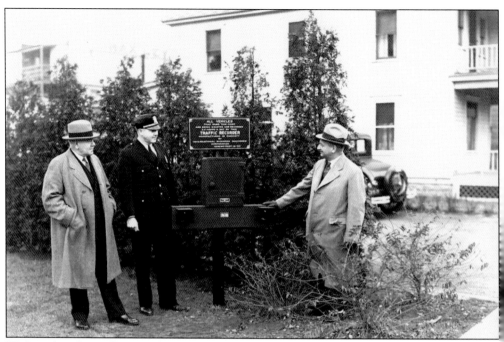

IBM produced a traffic recorder in 1936. The state-of-the-art counting device was guaranteed to only count cars, not cows or people. The prototype of the international traffic recorder was tested in Endicott with the assistance of a very cooperative police force, shown above.

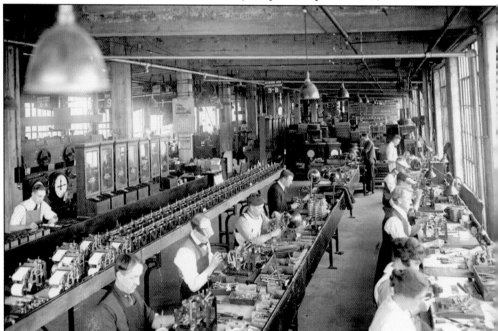

Another early product of ITR was the recording door lock. As part of the equipment in a watchman's station, it recorded the actual time a merchant's door was locked or unlocked, and who unlocked the door—"all profitable information for today's businessmen." The lock was considered a necessary protection for any business.

Harlow Bundy was memorialized in the April 1916 issue of ITR's *Time* magazine and in the *Binghamton Press*, which reported: "Mr. Bundy has done mankind a service it can never repay. He has taught the whole world the lesson of the value of time. He was a tower among his contemporaries. His keen perception, and big brain helped produce one of the most useful devices of the age, protecting employees and employers from the unfair use of time. . . . He will be reflected in our lives yea throughout all time."

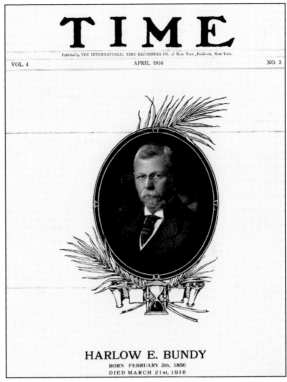

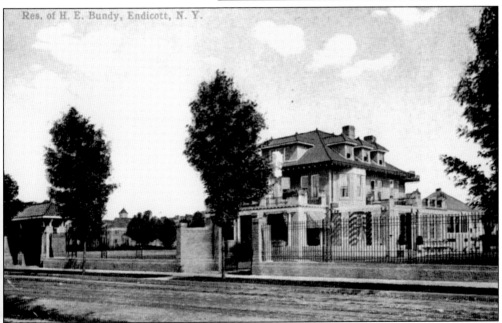

The residence of Harlow Bundy, on Park Street in front of Casino Park, was previously the home of C. Fred Johnson. It was remodeled to Bundy's own fancy, becoming one of the finest homes in Broome County. After his death, the house was purchased by the Endicott-Johnson Corporation. It became the Ideal Home Library, maintained and supported by EJ until the structure was demolished.

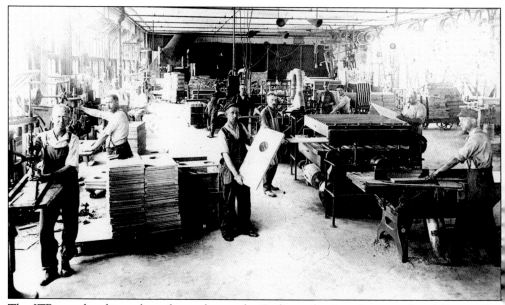

The ITR woodworking plant, located near the Endicott forging plant, produced fine-quality wood cabinets for the time recorders and clocks. This photograph is from the 1920 era. By the end of January 1989, the old cabinet shop had been torn down, along with two adjacent buildings. The plant had been one of the oldest of the IBM buildings. The vacant land was then used for parking lots.

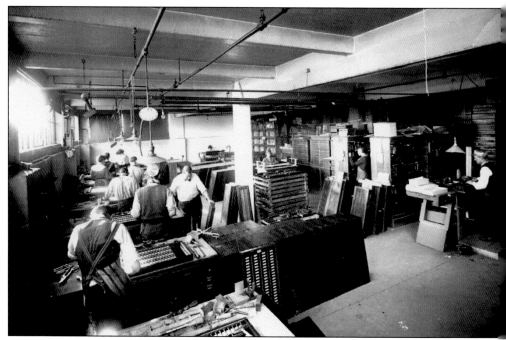

Timecard racks were made in the woodworking buildings on North Street. Very specialized machinery was used in the fabrication of the solid-wood racks.

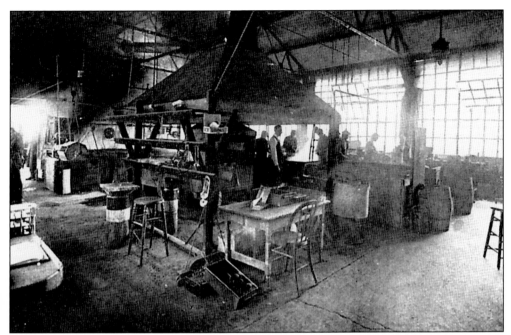

The plating department of IBM is pictured above in 1919, when most of the employees were men, and below in 1940, by which time women had secured a major place in the work force. This department polished and electroplated the time recorders and tabulating machines, and later, computer parts. In 1954, the newest IBM building housed a fully automatic system designed to continually treat waste liquids, recover metallic compounds, and dispose of chemical products.

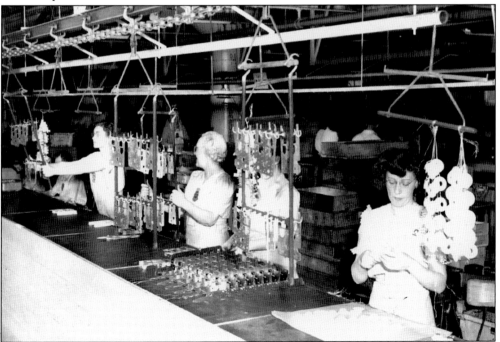

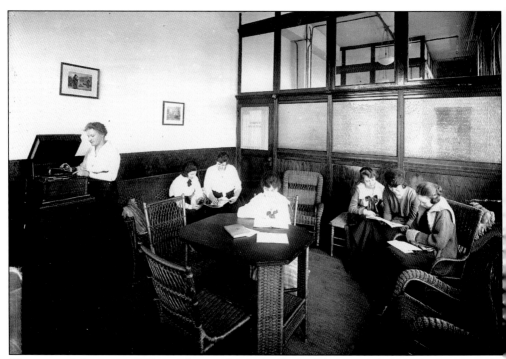

The women's lounge at ITR was designed specifically for "the young ladies who lived too far from home to leave for lunch," as it was described in an IBM booklet published in 1919. A Victrola was provided so "monotonies would be quickly abandoned when the little motor purred and played soothing music." Wicker furniture and reading material appropriate for women were also provided by the company.

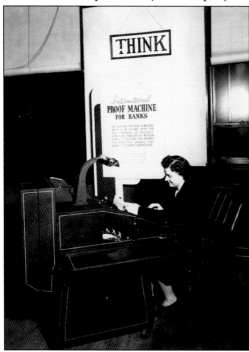

In 1934, the IBM 801 Bank Proof Machine was introduced. It listed and separated checks, endorsed them, and recorded totals

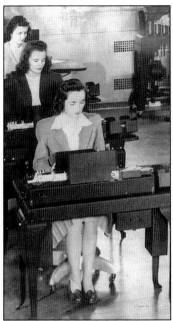 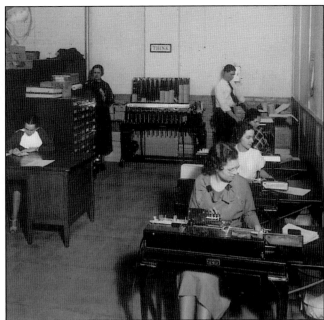

During the 1930s and 1940s, key-punch operators were nearly all women with typing skills. The left photograph shows IBM in 1948, and the right depicts the Endicott-Johnson tabulating department. Note the accepted sitting position and clothing of the era—almost identical in each office.

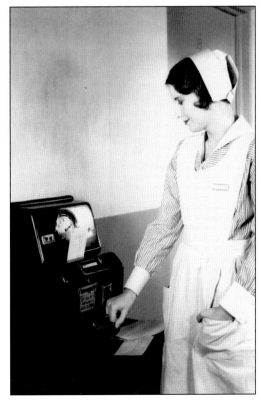

Every business and office needed a method for keeping track of employee hours; IBM provided the machines to fill the need. Here, a nurse follows the procedure to "shift the lever to record proper time" in 1925.

49

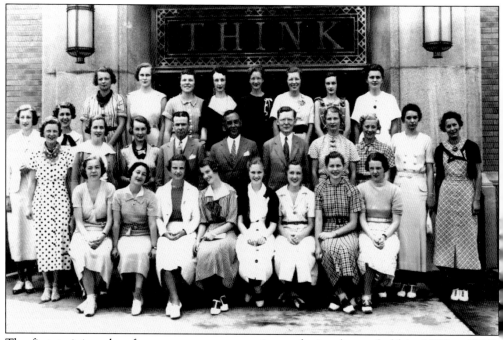

The first training class for women systems service professionals was held in 1935 at IBM's Endicott facility. Pictured is the graduating class, with a caption noted on the back: "System service girls . . . at last." The first female corporate vice president, appointed in 1943, was a member of this class.

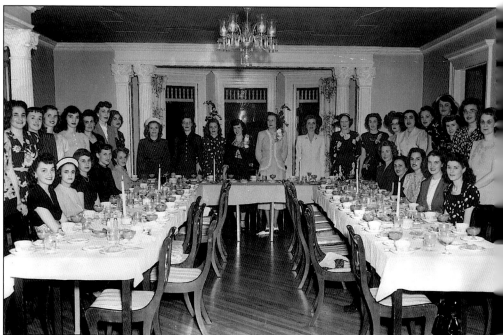

Between 1940 and 1943, during World War II, IBM doubled its manufacturing work force, and one-third of the company's 15,000 new employees were women. This photograph shows a party for key-punch girls in June 1948.

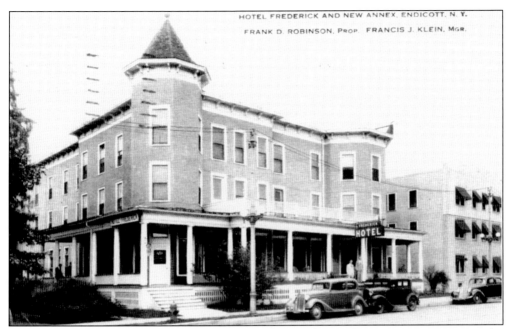

The Hotel Frederick was built in 1906 by the Endicott-Johnson Corporation, anticipating the need for accommodations, food, and entertainment for travelers. Both customers and salespeople from EJ and IBM made use of the facilities. In 1910, the hotel was host to an interesting billiards match that lasted several weeks. The "Clockmakers" of ITR and the "Shoemakers" of EJ squared off on Tuesday evenings. The first match was won by the Clockmakers—although every frame was said to have been close.

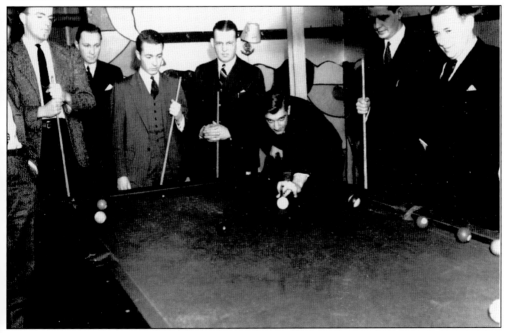

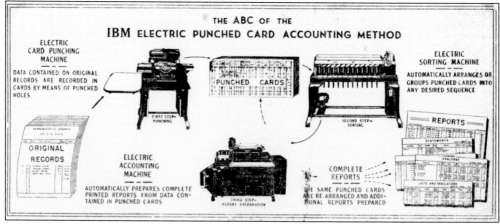

In the late 1920s, Thomas Watson Sr. promoted the advantages of punch-card machines compared to previous devices for data recording. Thereafter, the punch card became the most important and common method for information storage and retrieval. The photograph above, imprinted on a tabulating card, describes the punched-card accounting process.

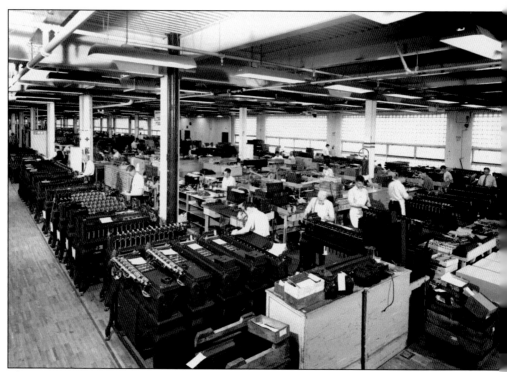

The IBM manufacturing plant produced thousands of key-punch machines and sorters, as shown in the 1948 photograph. Series E government bonds were also printed on IBM punch cards.

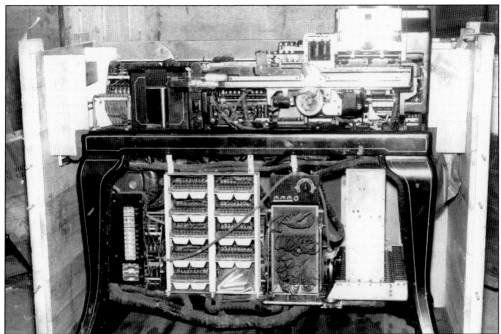

Revealing the "guts" of the Model 374 multiple-card punch, the above photograph shows the intricate wiring that service personnel had to be familiar with for repair and maintenance. Long before they went on the market, all electronic accounting machines passed an elaborate and thorough testing process. The device below was used for checking a machine's cables, c. 1944. Link Aviation was one of the companies that produced plugboards and cables for the IBM machines. This diverse business was a large factor in the post–World War II success of the Link Aviation company, which is now known worldwide for its flight-training devices.

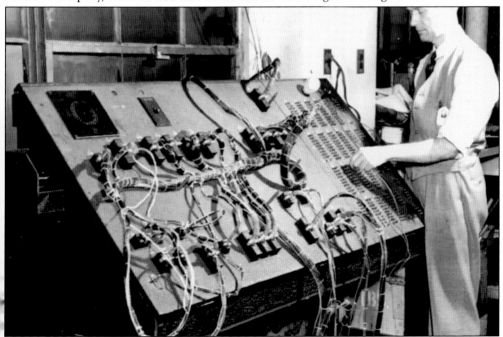

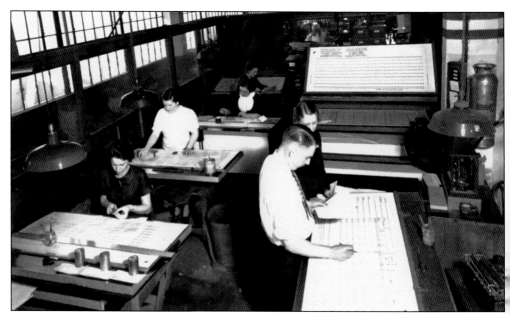

An important element in the punch-card process was the design of the cards, which were custom-made for each user. In 1928, the data capacity of the punch card was increased from 45 columns to 80 columns of information. IBM's layout department is pictured in 1935.

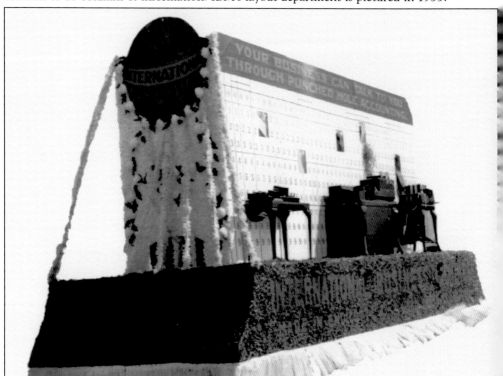

The punch card became so much a part of IBM and business life in general that its likeness was even used as a symbol on parade floats. The legend on this 1948 float reads, "Your business can talk to you through punched hole accounting."

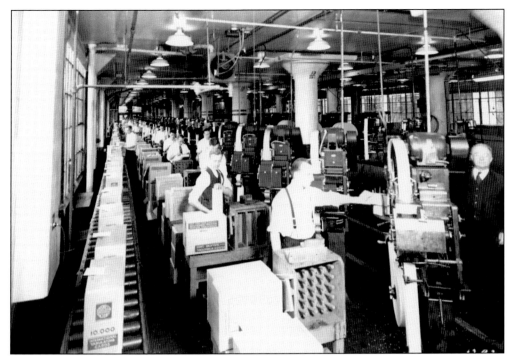

By 1937, IBM was making thousands of cartons of the tabulating cards to be shipped to countries around the world. The cards were tough and durable, but were marked with a warning that became part of household language: "Do not bend, fold, spindle or mutilate."

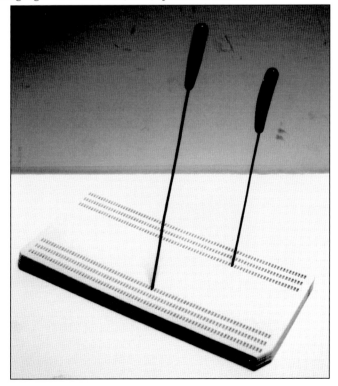

An important but forgotten tool of the punch-card era was the sorter key. This magic wand could be found in the pocket of every person who used the IBM card systems. It was, in effect, the troubleshooter, as it was constructed to find errors in a punched card. The stick was the exact size of a punched hole, and when inserted through a deck of cards, the sorter key could find an incorrect entry. The slightly melted red handle of one of the keys pictured came about when the useful life of the tool at IBM ended and it became a tester for doneness of cakes in Mom's kitchen.

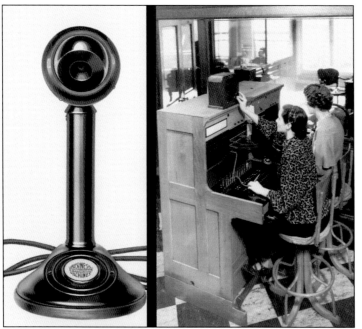

Telephones and switchboard systems were part of the IBM line of products used extensively in schools and industrial buildings. In 1927, IBM was also one of the first corporations to take advantage of the most modern phone service: the transatlantic radio phone between New York City and London. Watson noted that the new phone system was meritorious for saving time, labor, and money. Pictured are the IBM candlestick phone and switchboard *c.* 1930.

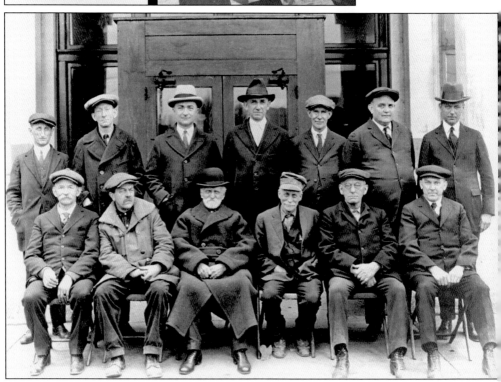

Formed in 1924, the IBM Quarter Century Club held its first meeting in Atlantic City, New Jersey. A total of 42 people received inscribed gold watches and chains from Thomas Watson, who called the group the "pioneers of IBM." By 1946, the number of members had grown to 341. In 1974, the Quarter Century Club's 50th-anniversary celebration was held in Endicott, with 8,500 people in attendance. Pictured above are some of the original club members in 1924.

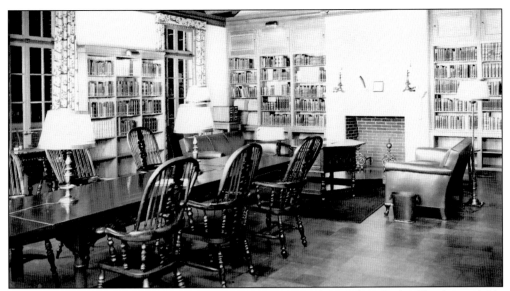

Established in Endicott in 1934, the IBM Library contained many hundreds of books available to employees. Located in building number 32 on the fifth floor, it was almost a hidden treasure. Wood-beamed ceilings, a stone fireplace, and mullioned windows added to the inviting atmosphere. Books on technical information, as well as those pertaining to culture, arts, and other topics, were included. Watson advised, "There is no saturation point in education." Over time, the gracious library became offices.

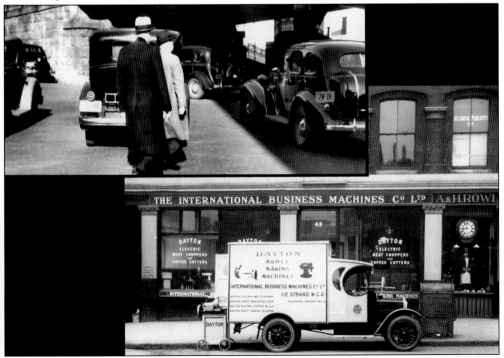

This composite photograph shows IBM on wheels in 1935. Above, T. J. Watson arrives at the rail station in Binghamton, where he will meet members of the One Hundred Percent Club sales convention. Below, an IBM truck delivers Dayton scales to a London dealer.

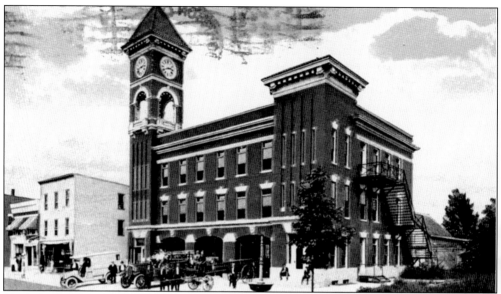

In 1912, the growing village of Endicott voted on a bond issue to finance construction of a $15,000 municipal building and fire station on Washington Avenue. Harlow Bundy stated that if the people of the village carried the proposition, he would donate a large Seth Thomas clock, costing more than $3,000, to be placed in the lofty tower. The tower also housed a bell that weighed over 1,000 pounds.

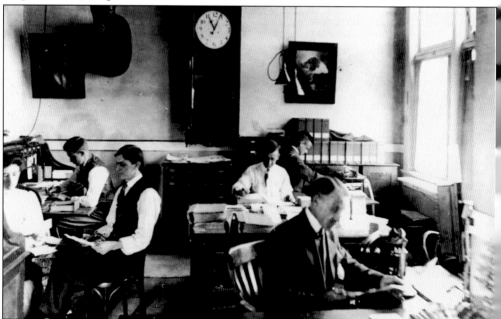

Many businesses in the Susquehanna Valley region started using ITR machines before ITR had even installed the devices in its own offices. The Larrabee-Deyo Truck Company traced its roots to 1882 and the making of cutters and wagons. In 1915, the company updated its product line and established a factory to make motor trucks. The Larrabee office also incorporated the modern accounting and timekeeping methods established by ITR. This photograph was taken at Larrabee c. 1920.

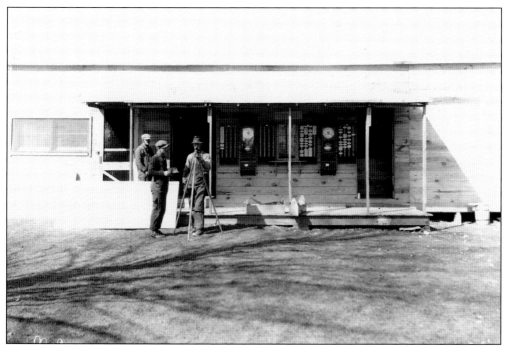

A local contractor and surveying company placed its IBM time recorders in a prominent position on the porch in front of its office in 1920.

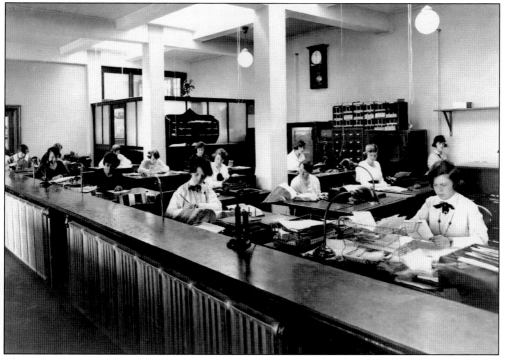

The great shoe-manufacturing firm of Endicott-Johnson put Endicott on the national map. EJ was one of the first major concerns to install ITR time clocks in all its facilities. In this 1920s EJ office, an ITR clock hangs on the back wall.

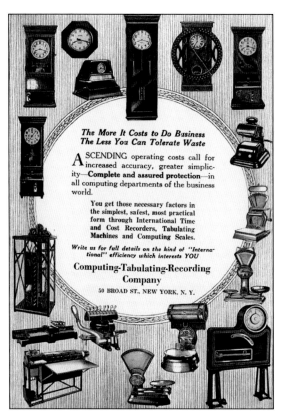

A January 1920 advertisement shows many of the items produced by the combined Computing-Tabulating-Recording Company.

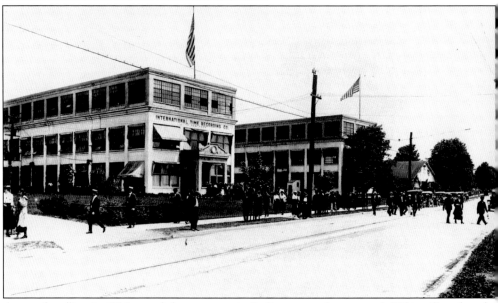

A news headline in 1912 noted that progress in Endicott was phenomenal. "This village has the greatest number of automobiles for any area its size in all of New York State. The day of an auto for every man is dawning." The total number of cars in Endicott was 39 at that time. By the date of this 1919 photograph, automobiles were so common that strict enforcement of parking near IBM had become necessary. A few decades later, many acres would be needed for employee vehicles.

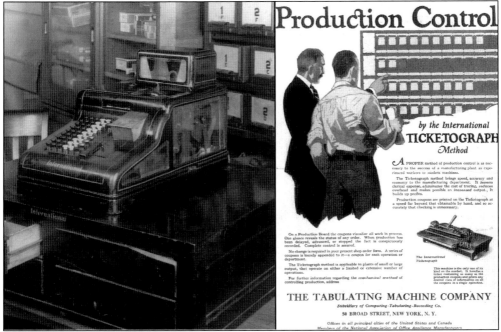

The Tabulating Machine Company produced a ticketograph in 1924 to speed a "proper method of production control." Advertised as the only machine of its kind on the market (right), it was guaranteed to assure complete control of production and status of any order. In 1942, the Ticketograph Division was acquired by the National Postal Meter Company. Also shown in this composite photograph is the International cash register, an IBM product.

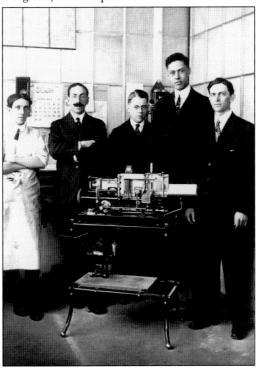

Admiring customers inspect their newest CTR office machines in 1918.

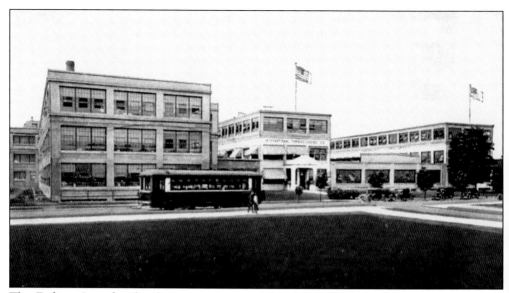

The *Endicott Record*, a local newspaper, reported in 1915: "ITR Employees Revolt Against Street Railway! As a result of alleged poor car service, and that the special cars provided for employees of the Time Recording Company are unfit to use, being dirty, old, weather beaten, cold, and in insufficient number to transport all employees, the employees will appeal to the Public Service Commission for relief from these conditions. These and other concerns led ITR people to boycott the trolley company and ride the Erie train to and from work. The street railway promised better service but never made good on previous occasions." Above is a streetcar in front of IBM on North Street. Below is a closer view of the street railway car.

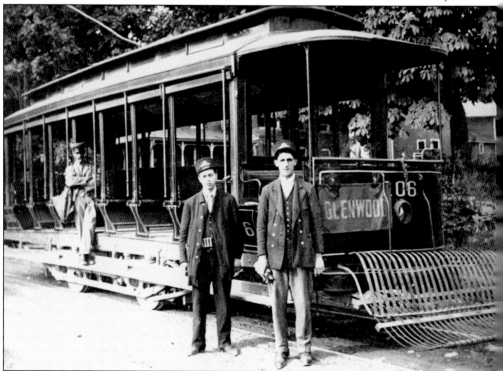

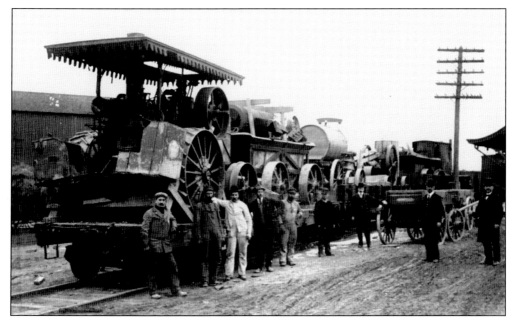

In 1908, workers and residents of Endicott and Lestershire demanded their elected leaders resolve the dust problem. Clouds of dirt from the roads were "ever injurious," and the trustees of 1908 responded as would politicians of today: "A uniform street sprinkling system can abolish dust but tax dollars are needed!" Doctors warned that the dreaded tuberculosis germs found in the dust were picked up by the wind, then spread into homes and lungs. The road equipment pictured was delivered to the villages by rail.

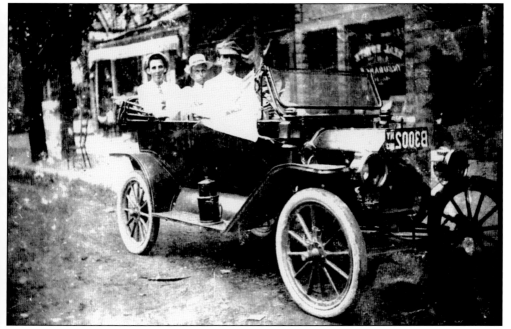

Many of the new arrivals in town used the "shoe leather route" to the North Street factories. But if necessary, Clark's Livery Service, a taxi business, transported ITR employees and visitors. Although the photograph was printed backwards, the license plate reads 1913.

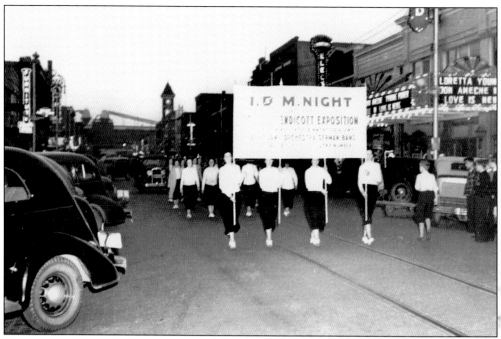

IBM promoted its products at every opportunity and participated in fairs, exhibitions, and parades all over the world, beginning in Endicott. Marching past the Strand Theater on Washington Avenue, a group of IBM employees displays details of the Endicott Exposition of 1940.

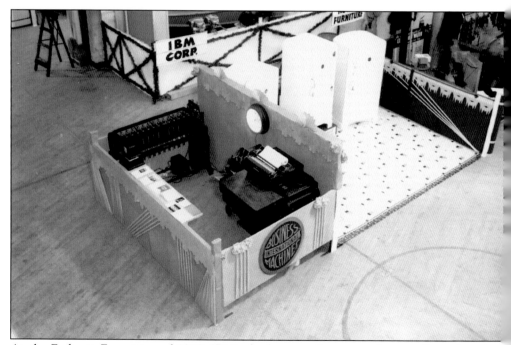

At the Endicott Exposition of 1940, IBM's display sat adjacent to the new line of modern refrigerators from Rouffs Furniture, which is now the well-known Olums Furniture.

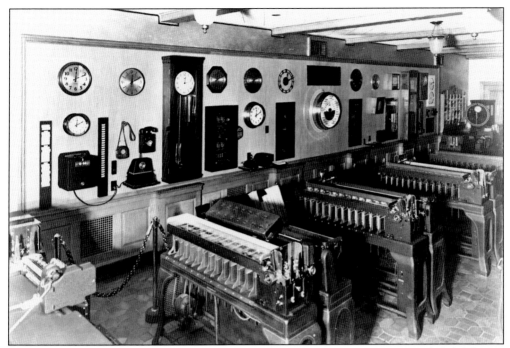

IBM's product line won a grand prize at the Sesquicentennial Exposition at Philadelphia in 1926. The display was similar to this one, which is set up for an Endicott show.

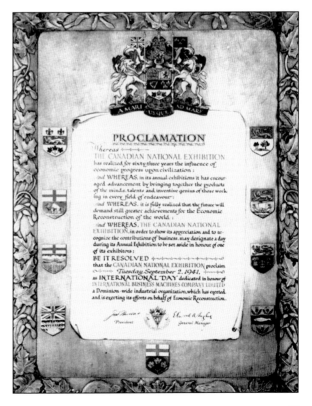

In 1941, the Canadian National Exposition designated Tuesday, September 2, as International Business Machines Day. The exposition praised IBM for its great progress in "exerting efforts toward Economic Reconstruction" after the Great Depression years.

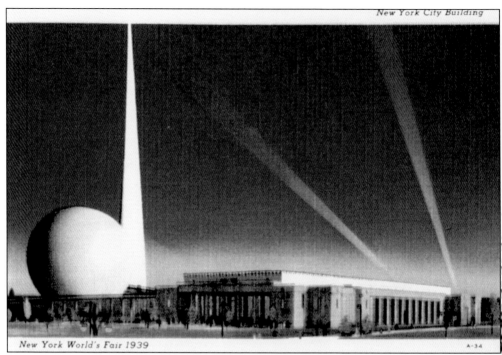

New York City was the site of the World's Fair from 1939 into 1940. IBM paid the expenses for Endicott employees and their spouses to travel to the city on the Erie Railroad for IBM Day at the fair in May 1940. Participants spent the entire weekend at the fair, with all costs absorbed by IBM. Employees later thanked their esteemed leader by donating a room devoted to the recuperation of children at Ideal Hospital in the name of T. J. Watson Sr.

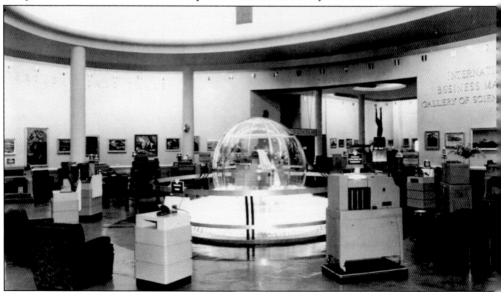

The IBM display at the 1939 World's Fair, held at Flushing Meadows Park in New York City was centered with a huge bubble containing an IBM 405 tabulator. Around the exhibit was displayed part of the corporate art collection—one painting from every country where IBM conducted business. A large array of new products completed IBM's show.

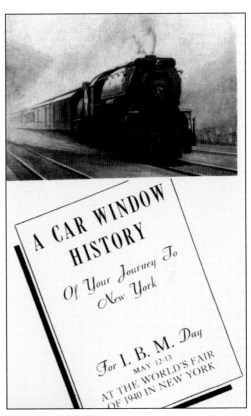

The special train filled with IBM employees traveling from Endicott to the New York City World's Fair experienced a major derailment before reaching its destination. Many people were injured and hospitalized. T. J. Watson visited every person hurt in the accident and promised a special IBM Day for everyone who was detained from attending the fair. At right is a copy of the official program for the IBM Day festivities. Below is a photograph of employees boarding the railroad cars at the Binghamton Station, along with an official guest ticket for the fair.

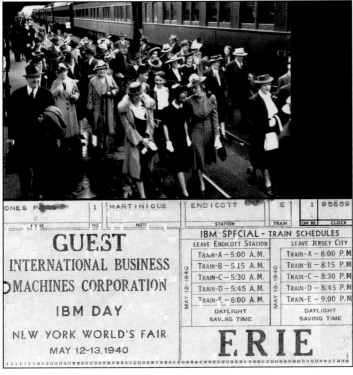

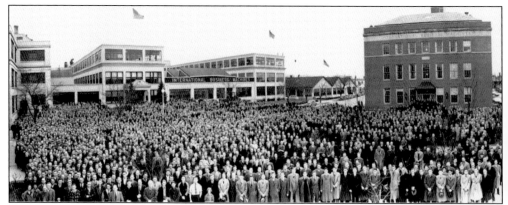

Twenty days before the start of the 1939 World's Fair, the entire work force at IBM Endicott assembled for a photograph to be displayed at the exhibit.

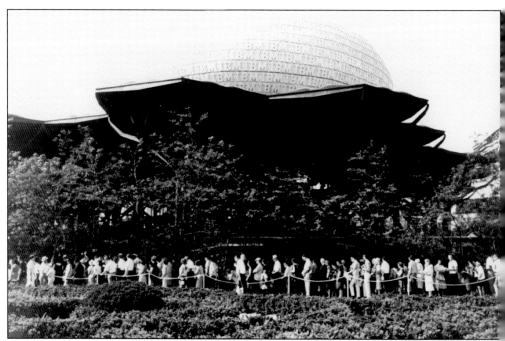

For the 1964 World's Fair in New York City, IBM again coordinated a magnificent exhibit. A specially designed building that closely resembled an IBM Selectric Type Ball was constructed. The exhibit and building cost $14 million. After the building was demolished, the exhibit traveled to various IBM locations around the country. During IBM Day at the fair, Pres. Dwight Eisenhower was a featured speaker.

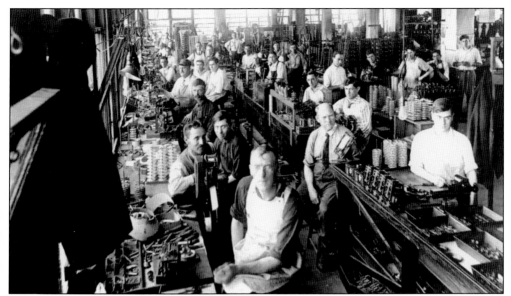

The Computing-Tabulating-Recording Company produced quality business equipment. A company assembly line is shown in 1916.

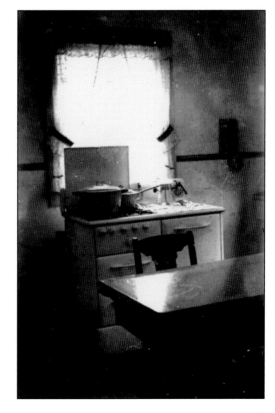

In a kitchen like this one, the homemaker probably spent time collecting and organizing manufacturers' coupons. IBM mailed thousands of money-saving coupons to private residences throughout the country. Each coupon was printed on a tabulating card exactly one-third the size of a standard card, to easily fit in a wallet.

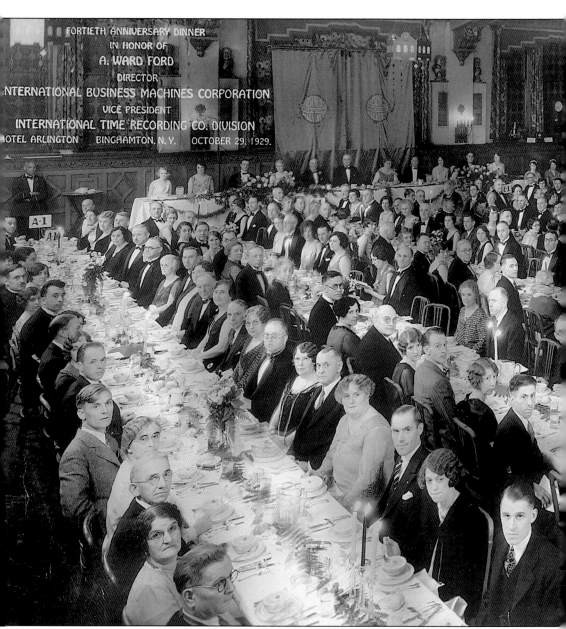

The 40th anniversary dinner in honor of A. Ward Ford was held on October 29, 1929. The sparkling art deco–designed ballroom of the Arlington Hotel in Binghamton was filled with employees. The product line was displayed around the room on balconies and fireplace

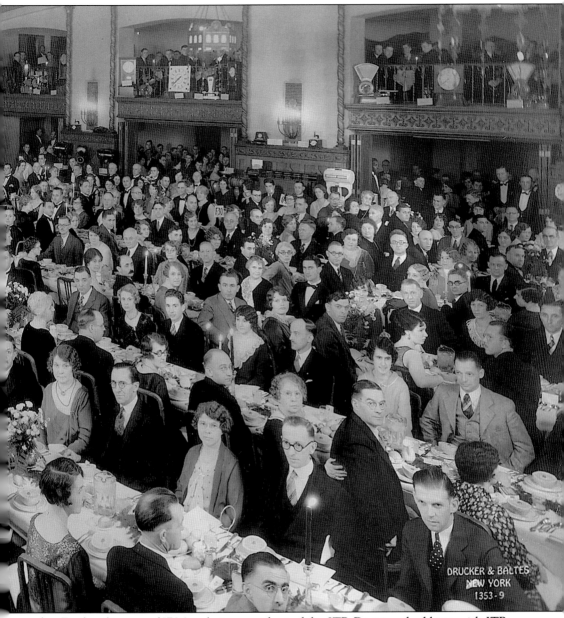

mantles. Ford, a director of IBM and vice president of the ITR Division, had been with ITR longer than any other employee.

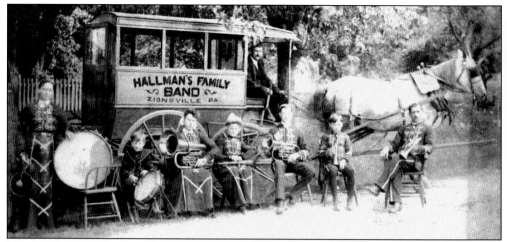

Lloyd C. Hallman became the leader of the IBM band in 1920. He gained musical experience early in life by participating in the Hallman's Family Band, a group led by his father, which traveled the countryside in a horse-drawn wagon (pictured above). Lloyd remained as director of the IBM band for more than 25 years.

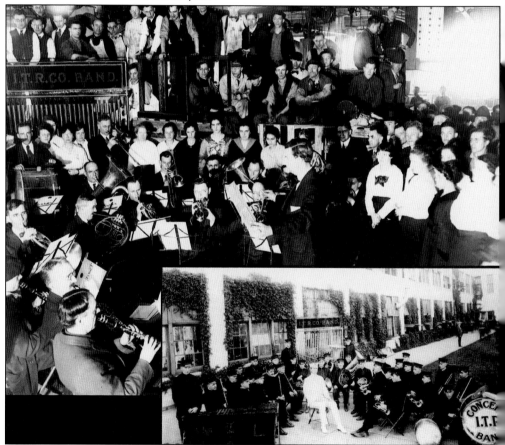

Outdoors or indoors, the company musicians inspired appreciation for culture and loyalty to the corporation. The above photographs of the ITR Company band were taken in the early 1900s.

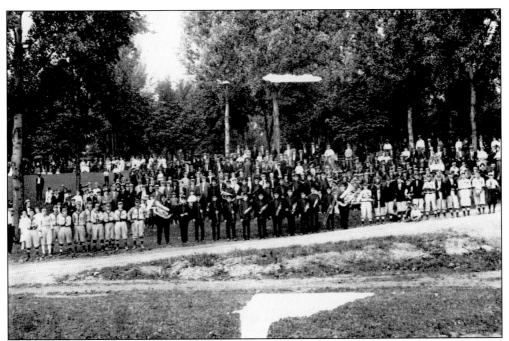

Community and company spirit were expressed in music when the ITR band formed in 1918. The group gave concerts inside the company buildings and every Wednesday at noon under the shade of a giant tree on the grounds. The ITR band played its first company convention with only 15 musicians; one year later, it had grown to three times that size. During the 1920s and 1930s, the band performed at all the One Hundred Percent Club sales conventions. From 1934 to 1940, the band participated in broadcasts on WNBF radio. And in the 1940s, the band played each day at Tent City in Endicott. Above, bands from Endicott-Johnson and IBM perform at a baseball game between the two corporate teams in Casino Park c. 1913. Below, the IBM youth band is pictured in the 1950s.

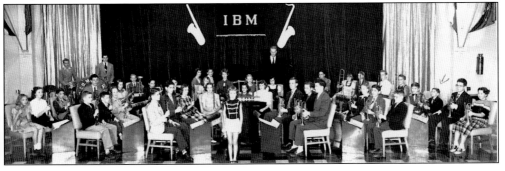

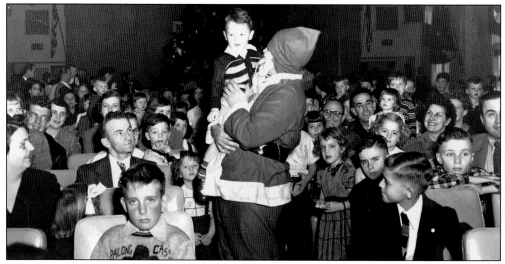

Each year, Christmas parties were held for all children of IBM employees. Santa arrived and gave gifts to each child. Activities at the IBM Country Club also stressed family participation. IBM Family Day began in 1950. By 1956, more that 50,000 people attended the free shows, which featured cyclists, acrobats, ventriloquists, and clowns. Music, mechanical carnival rides, and pony rides also entertained the crowds. Food was provided for all in attendance. Above is a scene from a Christmas party in the 1950s.

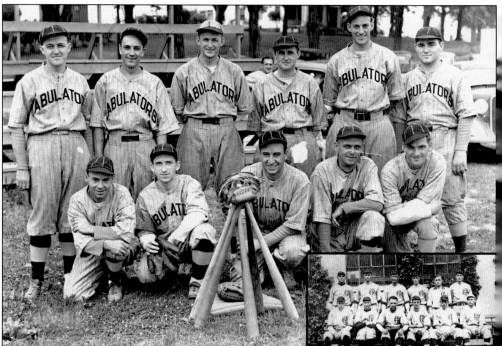

In 1919, the ITR Ball Tossers and women in the ITR office force planned a dance at the municipal building in Endicott. Funds raised helped defray costs of the team's entry into Industrial League competition. A fine party was reportedly held on May 29. The original ITR ball fields were near the factory buildings. The area also included a bandstand. This photograph shows the IBM Tabulators in the late 1940s. The 1919 ITR team is pictured in the inset.

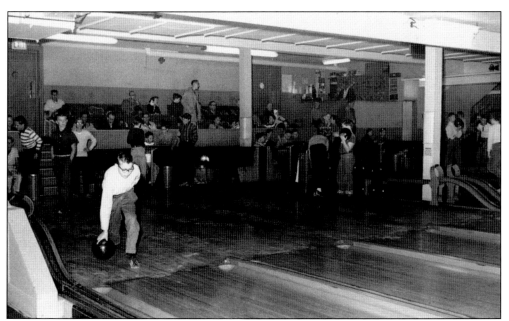

The IBM Country Club on Watson Boulevard (previously Green Street) was built with a professional bowling alley in the basement. Adult and children's activities were held in the spacious club. The photograph depicts the Junior Bowling Club in the 1950s. T. J. Watson believed leisure time from IBM should be spent as part of the IBM family. Picnics, sports, movies, classes, and clean entertainment were all available to employees.

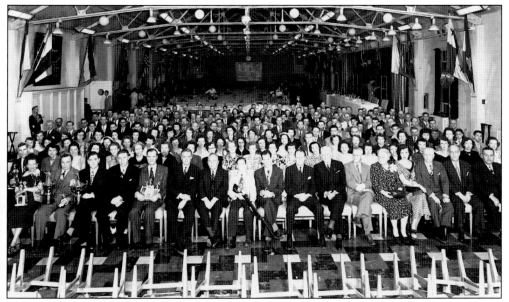

Huge trophy dinners were held at the end of each season to recognize IBM's winning teams. Trophies were presented to every individual . . . no matter how long the celebration took. All events were dry, as no liquor was ever permitted at any IBM function. In 1939, sports history was made when the IBM Country Club allowed the formation of girls' softball teams. A local newspaper, the *Binghamton Press*, reported of the women's athletic competition, "The unusual spectacle attracted a large gallery of spectators."

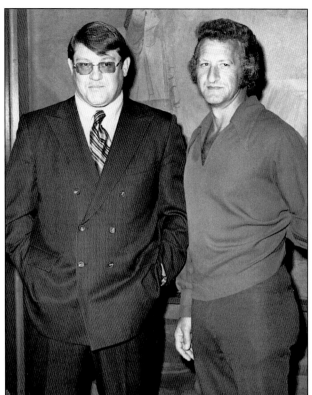

The IBM Country Club spared no expense in luring impressive athletes to speak at the trophy dinners. Alex Karras (left) and Bob Uecker are seen at the club just before Karras's inspirational talk to attendees.

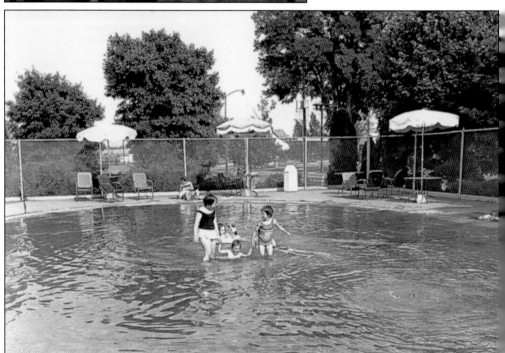

The country club also featured a full-size swimming pool and a child-friendly wading pool next to a fenced playground for toddlers. Lessons were provided by trained swimming instructors.

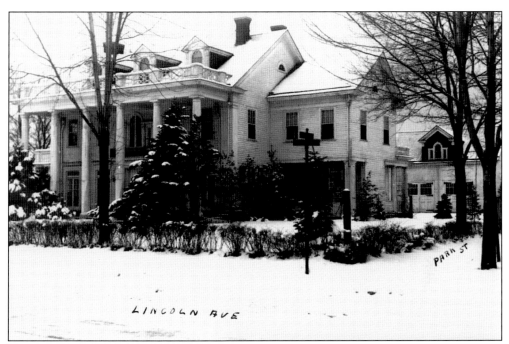

The grand Bowes Estate above—now known as Colonial Hall—was built in 1904, and once belonged to an employee of Endicott-Johnson. By the 1930s, ownership had passed to IBM, and Watson was interested in using it to found a tuition-free college as part of IBM. He wanted IBM to be the first company to own and operate a college. However, with some persuasion, Watson changed his mind and sold the Bowes Estate to Syracuse University. Shortly after World War II, Watson helped start the Triple Cities College. The school eventually became Harpur College, part of the State University of New York (SUNY) system at Binghamton University. Colonial Hall is now the Endicott Visitors Center. Watson also considered turning the Bowes mansion into a day-care center for children of IBM employees, but instead he chose to establish the IBM Children's Club in a log cabin located in a beautiful wooded setting at the foot of the IBM Glen near the Homestead. The club is pictured on the right in the 1950s.

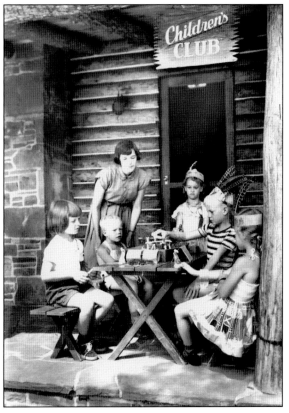

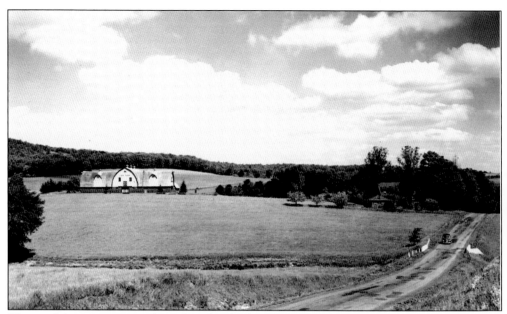

Watson did not give up easily on his idea for founding an IBM-sponsored college in the Triple Cities. He owned several "show farms" in New York state, and one was located on 300 acres in the Endwell section of the town of Union. He offered the site to the State University of New York for construction of a major campus, but SUNY opted to build in Vestal instead. Pictured above is the Endwell farmland, and below, a pair of impressive horses raised there. The Maine-Endwell Senior High School on Farm to Market Road is now located on part of this farm.

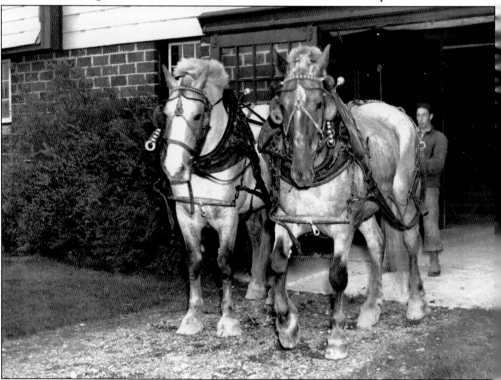

IBM donated a 52-acre tract of the farm in Endwell to the town of Union, along with a check for $100,000 to develop a park and recreation area. Highland Park is the result. The park includes an authentic Herschell carousel, which was originally donated by Endicott-Johnson in 1925 to En-Joie Park in Endicott. It is the only one of the local carousels to have been moved from its original site. Later, 162 acres of the tract were sold for residential development. Three lots were sold to local churches. Pictured to the right is a map of the area; below, the Highland pool and bathhouse that overlook the new housing projects.

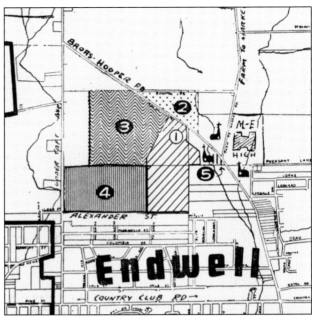

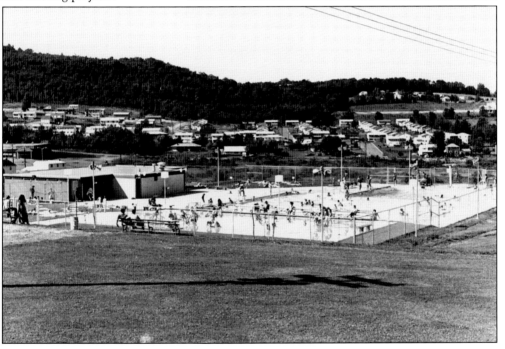

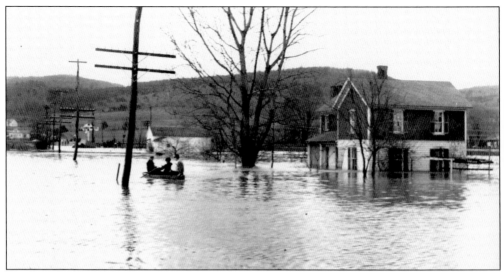

The Susquehanna River Valley has always presented the challenge of flood survival. Endicott was inundated by water in 1902, and in 1910, a news account declared, "'Casino Flats' is already disappearing under water as are the traditional marsh areas." Major floods occurred in 1935 and again in 1936. WPA workers were called to assist in 1935, when the Endicott Water Company was disabled. IBM gave $5,000 and tabulating equipment to the Red Cross disaster fund. In the flood of 1936, the company again offered equipment and trained operating personnel to the relief effort, and paid workers for lost time. IBM also donated the services of its engineering department to clean and repair household appliances and vacuum cleaners damaged by flood silt. Seen above is an Endicott Street fit only for boats in 1936. In 1960 a "freak storm" caused extensive flood damage to Endicott and the IBM plants. Mountains of mud collapsed a building wall, and elevator shafts became waterfalls. Pictured below is an area of floating office equipment from building 46.

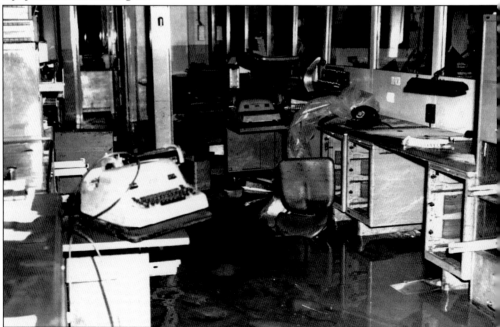

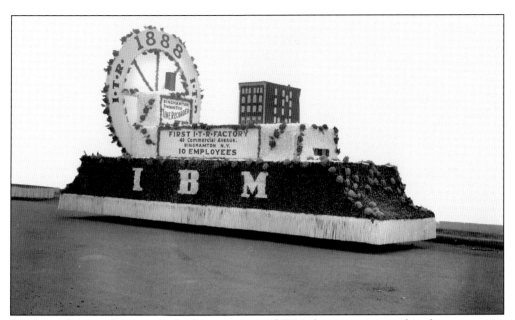

Local parades were frequent in the last century, and IBM always participated in the community events. The company's floats were elaborate productions; this IBM showpiece celebrated the origins of the time recorder at the Bundy factory on Commercial Alley in Binghamton.

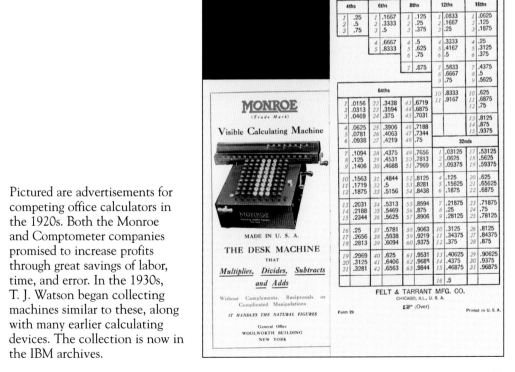

Pictured are advertisements for competing office calculators in the 1920s. Both the Monroe and Comptometer companies promised to increase profits through great savings of labor, time, and error. In the 1930s, T. J. Watson began collecting machines similar to these, along with many earlier calculating devices. The collection is now in the IBM archives.

81

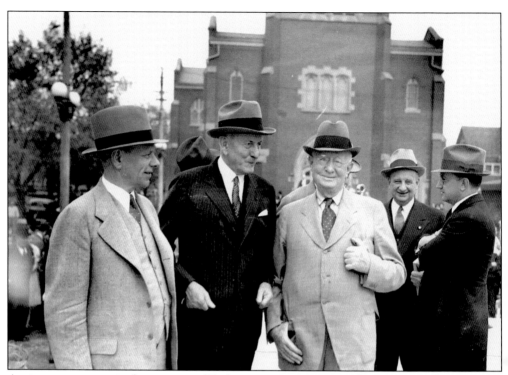

An important event in the progress of Endicott was construction of a new post office. In 1936, both T. J. Watson of IBM (second from left) and George F. Johnson of EJ (third from left) participated in the dedication of the new postal building. Crowds of people and automobiles lined the streets on the occasion. The picture below shows the exterior of mercantile establishments on Washington Avenue during an era of industrial prosperity.

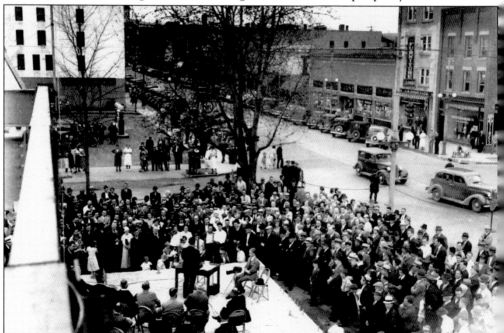

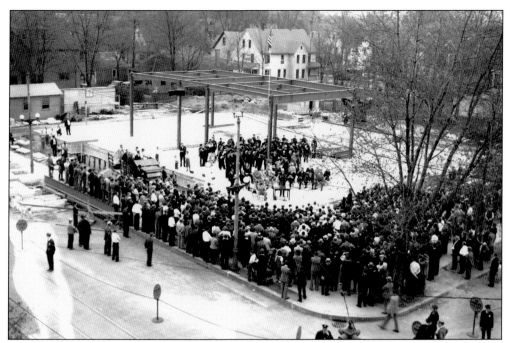

The dedication of the new post office was of major significance to the growth of Endicott. At the time of this photograph, there were still trolley tracks on the streets of the village.

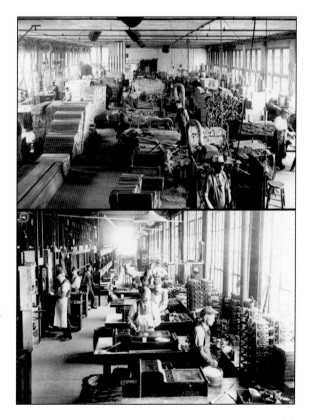

Skilled carpenters were always needed at the woodworking shops of ITR/CTR/IBM. This composite photograph shows the woodworking and cabinet shops c. 1919. Every clock case, packing case, card rack, tool cabinet, ribbon spool, pendulum stick, glass molding, and casting pattern was made in this production area. More than 100,000 feet of special kiln-dried wood was used each month. The department manager, Mr. Winsor, was complimented in 1919 on the department output and his personal record of having never rung in late or taken a single sick day in his 23 years of service with ITR.

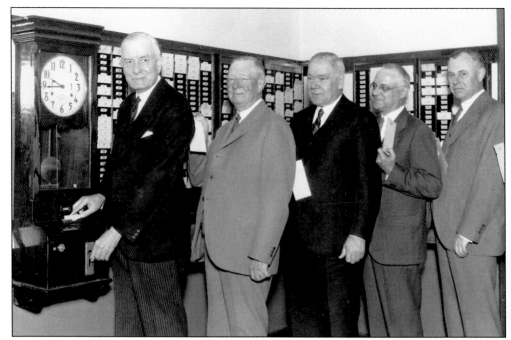

In 1932 T. J. Watson Sr. leads a group of fellow industrialists as he introduces them to the latest time-recording system. George F. Johnson, president of the Endicott-Johnson Shoe Manufacturing Corporation, is second in line, showing his timecard.

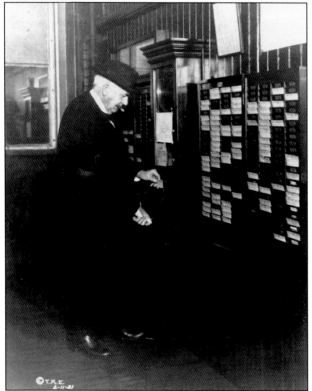

This IBM time clock performs celebrity duty in 1921. Thomas A. Edison, inventor of the phonograph, light bulb, and the motion picture projector, seems intent on working the new timekeeping device. T. J. Watson Sr. called Edison "one of the greatest benefactors of mankind in all history."

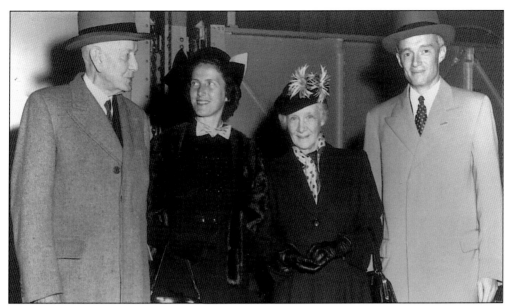

The IBM World Headquarters Building, located at 590 Madison Avenue in New York City, was dedicated in 1938, and is pictured below in 1948. This division of IBM published the *World Trade Journal* in three languages, beginning in 1937. Arthur K. Watson, the second son of T. J. Sr., became president of World Trade in 1956. He built the division into a dominant force in foreign business; by the 1960s, IBM had installed 90 percent of the computers in Europe. Arthur was awarded the French Legion of Honor in 1956, the third member of the Watson family so honored. He was also appointed United States ambassador to France in 1970. In the late 1960s, World Headquarters was moved to Armonk, New York. In the photograph above, T. J. Watson Sr. stands on the far left and Arthur Watson is on the far right.

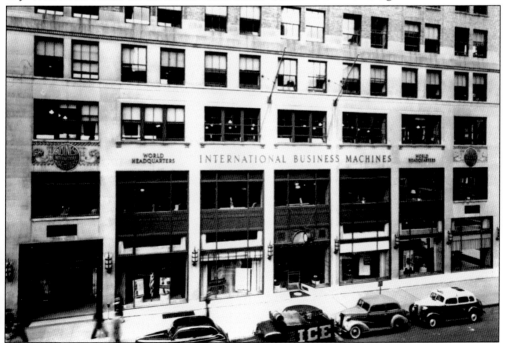

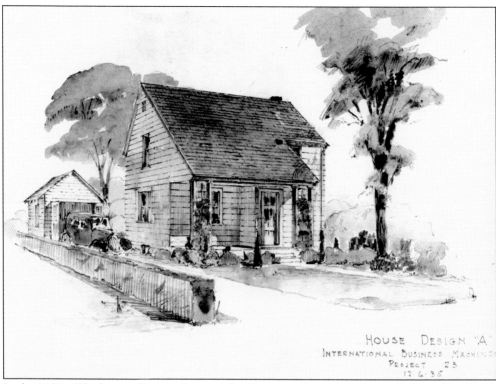

In the 1930s, IBM began planning housing developments for its employees. Endicott Highlands made it possible for employees to realize the "dream of every man": home ownership. In 1940 a group of grateful owners presented T. J. Watson Sr. with a large album containing photographs of all the homes in the development and the families who resided there. A model home design is pictured above, and actual homes are shown below.

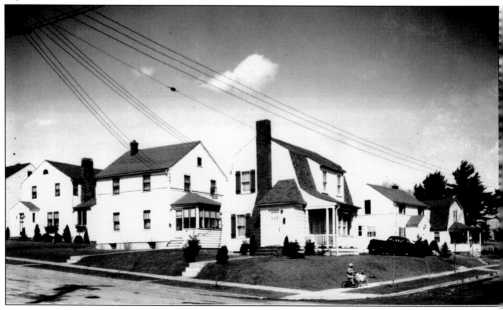

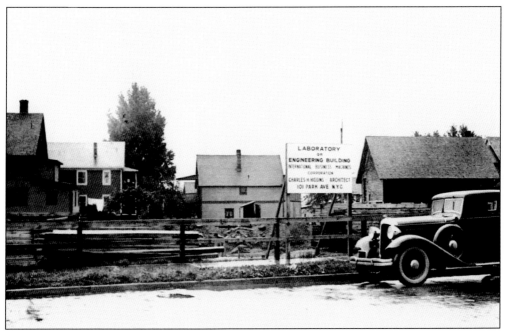

T. J. Watson Sr. used his considerable salesman skills to talk a bank into loaning IBM $25,000 to build an engineering laboratory. He believed research and engineering were the heart of the IBM business. The above photograph shows the Endicott site in 1932, prior to the laboratory's construction, and the image below shows the completed facility in 1933. By 1940, the laboratory was acknowledged as having "more scientific ability per square foot than any other building in America." The North Street facility became a landmark symbolizing industrial progress.

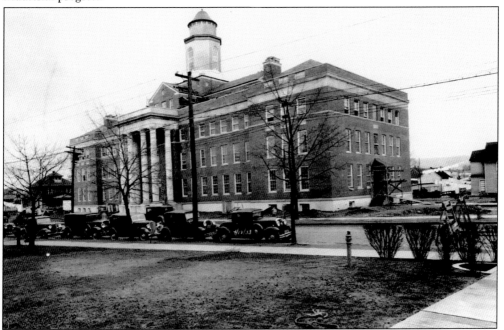

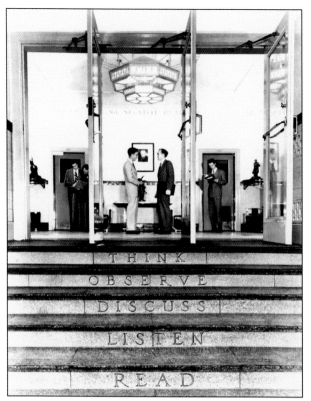

Progressive learning opportunities for employees became a priority for IBM. By 1928, the money spent on education was a major part of the corporation budget. In 1936, IBM began offering education to customers. The IBM schoolhouse and engineering laboratory was dedicated in 1933. The entry steps pictured at left are engraved with T. J. Watson Sr.'s "Five Steps to Knowledge": Read . . . Listen . . . Discuss . . . Observe . . . Think. Below is an exterior photograph of the building.

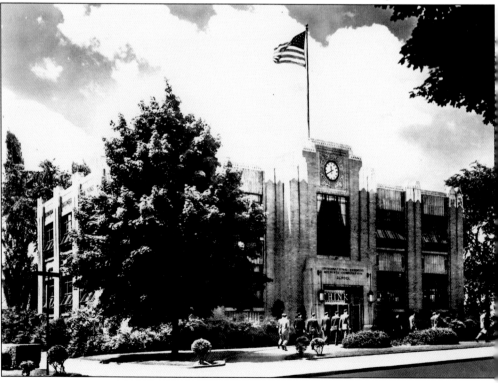

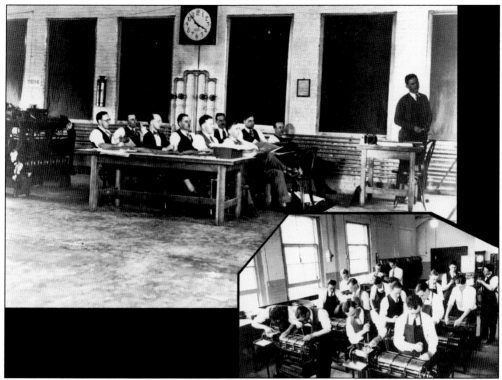

Pictured in 1928 is an IBM class reaching for the brass ring of advancement in corporate America. Students are shown working in the classroom (top) and in the hands-on "engineering" room (inset).

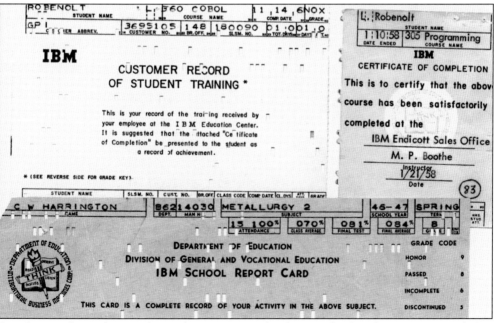

Certificates of completion of attendance at IBM schools, records of student training, and IBM school report cards were all printed on the company tabulating cards.

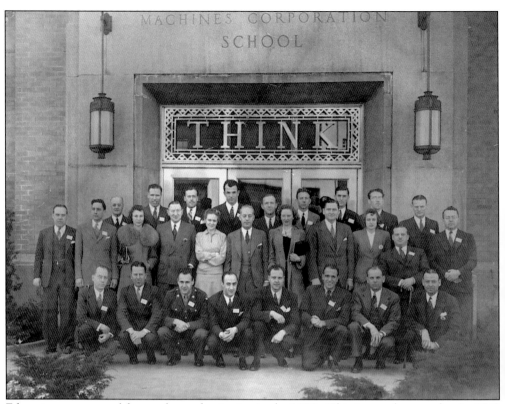

Education was stressed for employees beginning in the 1920s. This image shows a class in 1942 in front of the IBM school.

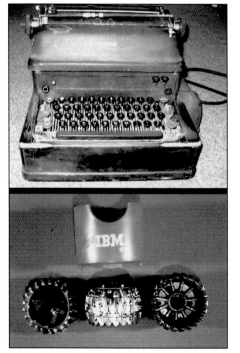

IBM acquired Electromatic Typewriters Inc. of Rochester, New York, in 1933. The purchase provided IBM with an office machine that was needed by businesses everywhere as well as technical information useful in tabulator printers. In 1941 the model 04 electric typewriter was introduced. The Selectric typewriter was developed in 1961, and presented a revolutionary invention: a golf ball–sized element that could change the typing font. It was an instant success. These photographs show the early electric typewriter and the 1961 font elements.

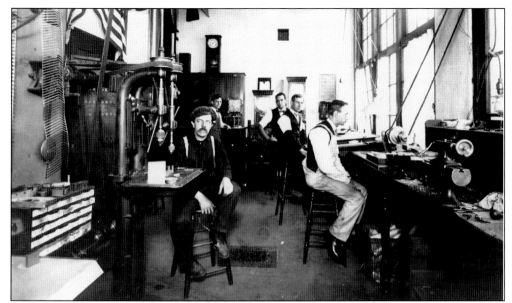

In 1918, ITR provided an Apprentice Division to train machinists, where preference was given to sons of company men. The boys had to be between the ages of 16 and 18, have the equivalent of a common school education, be of good habits, and have unimpaired sight and hearing. By 1938 IBM reinvented this idea and offered a prestigious program for local high school boys in apprentice toolmaking courses. Those selected to attend were usually graduates of Union-Endicott or North High School in Binghamton. Students who excelled in technical courses in high school were eligible. Only 15 to 20 students a year were chosen for the intensive three-year training. Both practical machine tool operation and classroom work in the manufacturing of tools and tool design were offered. The photographs show a 1918 training room (above) and a graduating class in 1938 (below).

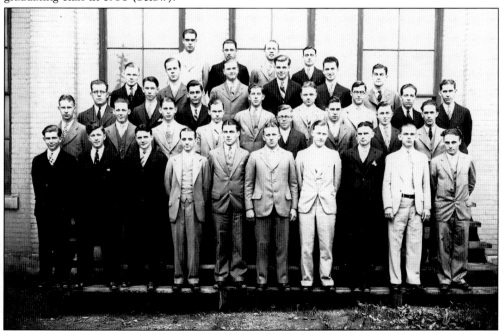

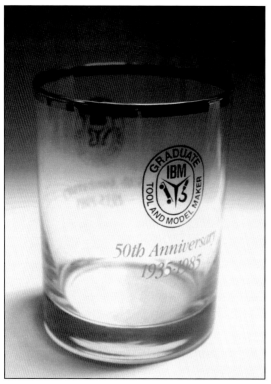

The 50th anniversary of the IBM tool and model maker program was celebrated in 1985. Two thousand souvenir glasses were created for the festivities; each was imprinted with the toolmakers' symbols and the anniversary dates, and was rimmed in gold. The goblets were delivered, but upon viewing a sample, an executive declared that the crystal container resembled a highball glass, and the appearance of possible use for alcohol would not be tolerated. Fifty cartons of glasses were relegated to the garbage so that employees would be saved from getting the "wrong message" regarding IBM temperance policies.

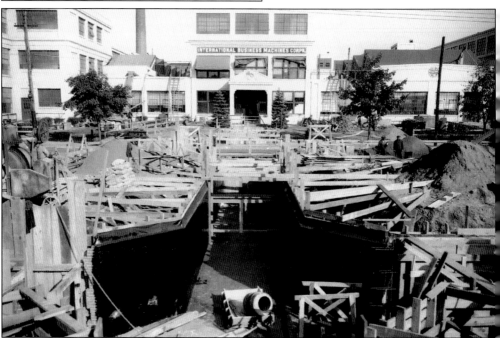

As the number of buildings in the IBM complex grew, it became imperative to have safe and easy access from one to another in any kind of weather. A series of tunnels was constructed underground, and enclosed bridges were built over the street. This photograph shows the tunnel under North Street before completion.

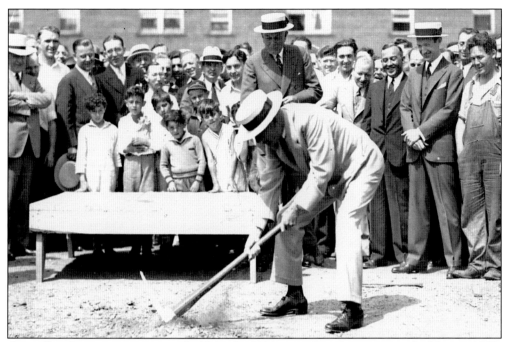

Groundbreaking ceremonies were held for the IBM research and engineering building in 1932. Watson planned to make IBM "Depression proof" by continual improvement in the product line and the addition of new machines. A. Ward Ford performs the honors with the pick as Watson watches; both are wearing fashionable straw hats.

Although the Depression reached into nearly every business and home, during the 1930s IBM expanded. The sales force was doubled, new buildings were constructed, and the company made parts that were not yet needed, all to provide steady employment. When IBM received a contract from the government for machines to handle Social Security records, the company already had all the parts necessary to fill the order promptly. This building is under construction in 1933.

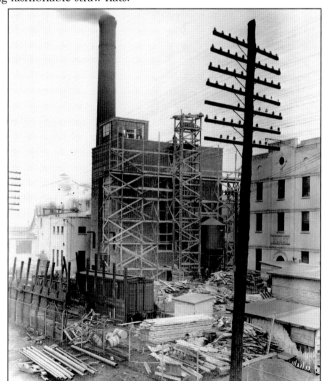

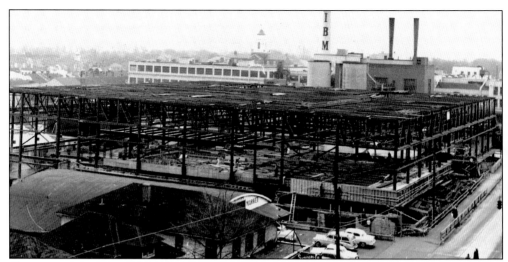

Construction continued in 1941. A building on North Street was designed with more glass brick than any other building in the world—a total of 75,445 glass blocks. Squares were stuffed with spun glass where non-glare diffusion was needed. One million hard-maple wood blocks measuring 2 by 2 by 12 inches were laid by hand for the floors. Cork was used between the floors to reduce noise and vibration. The cornerstone contains two etching plates by artist John Taylor.

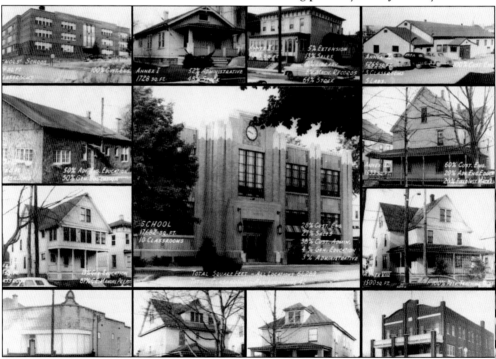

In 1942, IBM held a great dedication party for its newest building. Opera stars Lily Ponds and James Mellon attended the huge rally, which ended with a banquet for 3,000 people at the country club. After the war, the corporation continued to grow rapidly and space was needed immediately. Existing buildings throughout the Southern Tier were rented or purchased and converted into IBM offices for administration, engineering, sales, and record storage. This composite view shows a few of these sites.

Three
IBM AND THE WAR YEARS

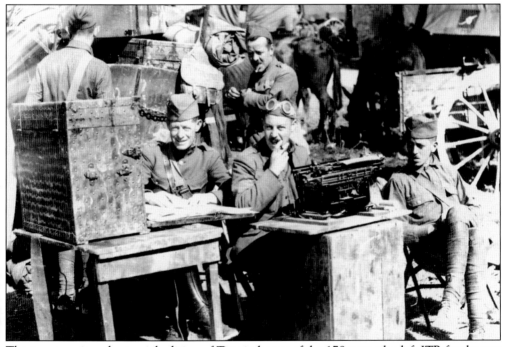

The company issued a special edition of *Time* in honor of the 178 men who left ITR for the war in 1918. As a further tribute to the servicemen, the corporate service flag bore 178 stars; that number was later expanded to 204. ITR was affected more than other local business, as it had a large shipment of goods ready for foreign destinations when war broke out, and most of the orders were canceled. In this image, a record-keeping unit uses the "most modern" equipment: a typewriter. During this time, Endicott residents and corporations were issued a warning from the government: "War work for the birds! Even though there are shortages, don't shoot pigeons for food! They could be part of the army defense system. Carrier pigeons are trained by the Army Signal Corps in many parts of U.S. including New York State. Sometimes birds are the best way to communicate on a battlefield."

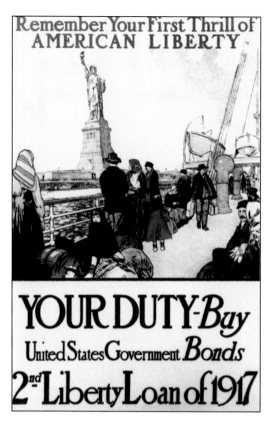

War fund-raising projects received the support of the entire work force in the Endicott ITR plant. The company generously donated to the Liberty Loans, Victory Loans, Red Cross, Canteen Fund, and U.S. War Work Fund as an expression of loyalty and sacrifice at home. All ITR facilities were offered to the government for war projects.

When World War II was declared, IBM again offered all of its facilities for the war effort. Support of the war was expressed on everything the company printed. The class graduation book for 1941, issued on IBM tabulating cards, had the "We All" slogan on the cover, along with the class motto of "Service for Victory." All pay statements were issued with information about war loan deductions. Note the weekly pay on this stub was $52.11.

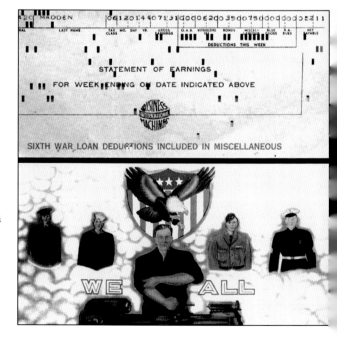

IBM developed Mobile Machines Record Units using electric accounting machines housed in trailer trucks that traveled wherever the troops were stationed, in all theaters of war. Quick operational data was needed to direct modern warfare, including troop movements and personnel payments. The U.S. Army first sent Sgt. Leonard Robenolt to college in California to train on the latest IBM mobile devices, then to the Philippine Islands to dodge bullets and malaria, and compute data for the military. In another theater, headlines in national newspapers read, "Patton Drive across France Aided by IBM Machines." Information and logistical data for Gen. George S. Patton Jr., derived from IBM statistics, helped determine the successful drive across France by U.S. forces. The photograph at right depicts Sergeant Robenolt; below, an Army truck contains IBM machines.

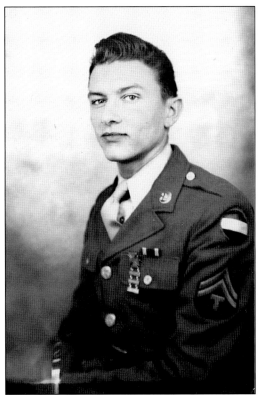

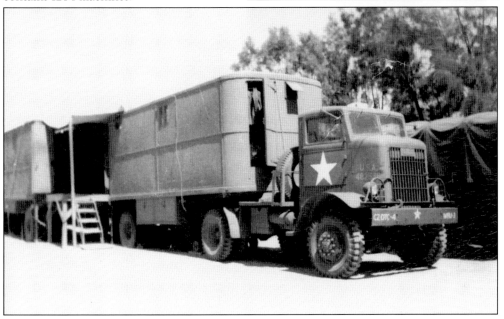

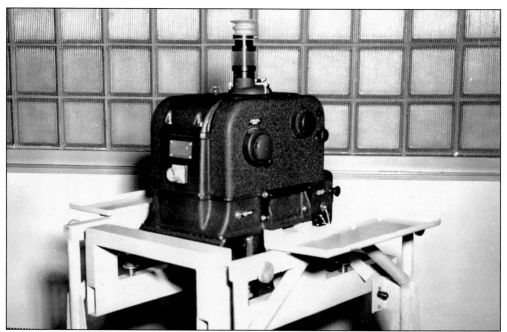

IBM's engineering laboratories worked on 99 top-secret military research and development projects. War profits were limited to less than 1.5 percent, and that amount went to help widows and orphans of IBM's war dead. This photograph shows a bomb sight made in Endicott.

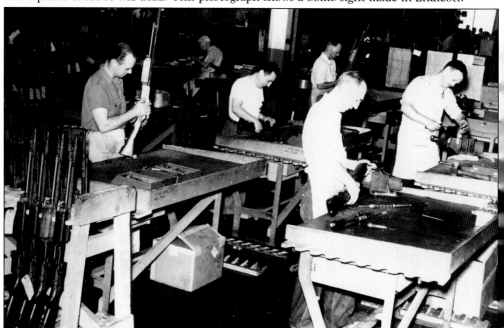

Nearly every soldier who went through gunnery training was familiar with the .30-caliber carbine, the Browning automatic rifle, and the .50-caliber machine gun. IBM manufactured parts of all three weapons. In February 1942, the company began working on a new building placed on the site of a North Street parking lot; by September, the new factory had to be ready to manufacture guns. At this time, 80 percent of IBM was devoted to war work.

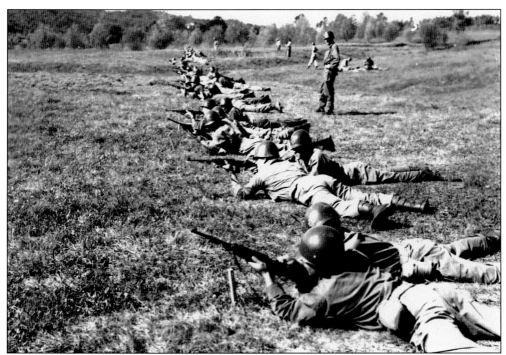

Above, troops practice with munitions manufactured by IBM. During the World War II era, IBM doubled its work force. In 1941, the total payroll was $10 million; by 1942, it had increased to $20 million. T. J. Watson Sr. made sure all IBM workers in the armed forces received a quarter of his IBM salary, up to the maximum of $1,000 per year, plus life insurance and rehabilitation services for the disabled. Watson further contributed to the war effort by loaning his 100-foot schooner to the U.S. Coast Guard at no cost.

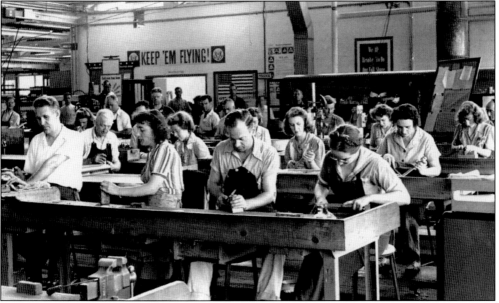

Women became important to the war effort by filling positions in factories and assembly lines. This work force is at IBM Endicott, where war posters adorn the walls.

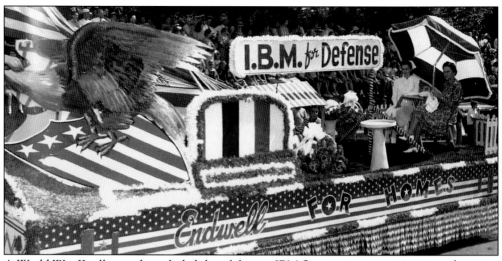

A World War II rally parade included this elaborate IBM float to inspire patriotism and support for the war bond drives. IBM also sponsored major theatrical stars to attend local bond drive banquets. Lily Ponds arrived in 1942 as an honored guest at the Lower Country Club, the same year actress Irene Dunne spoke at a war bond dinner. More than 3,000 people attended the dinner and war rally parade. After the war, dignitaries continued to arrive in Endicott. General of the Army George C. Marshall, author of the Marshall Plan for postwar recovery and a former secretary of state, was the featured speaker at a One Hundred Percent Club convention in 1949. His inspiring presentation included thanks to IBM employees for their exceptional war work. Pictured below are programs from two of the events.

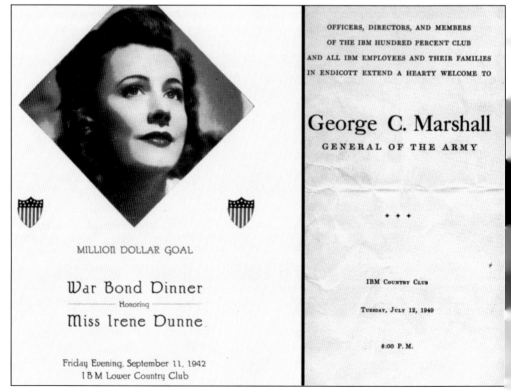

Women not only worked in the factories during the war, but also became valuable members of the military. They were occasionally photographed in poses that today would be considered stereotyped. The woman at right saved memorabilia (pictured below) from her tour of duty, including printed information on "corset conservation tips" and a tag to be worn over a button proclaiming, "I helped the over seas cigarette fund" sponsored by Binghamton American Legion Post 80.

CORSET CONSERVATION TIPS TO PASS ON TO YOUR CUSTOMERS

1. Have every foundation garment—including brassieres—fitted to your figure so it will do a good supporting job without undue strain at any point.

2. Wear foundation garments alternately, so they can have rest between wearings and wear every garment fairly frequently, because the rubber needs exercise as well as rest to keep lively a long time.

3. Keep them clean—frequent tubbings prolong their life; perspiration and grime ruin them.

4. Never use an iron on elastic sections.

5. Make minor repairs promptly—never use a safety pin for emergency repair because it may rip the fabric. If the repair job is beyond your skill, bring the garment in to the store for mending.

6. Buy only what you need — hoarding is impractical as well as unpatriotic because the rubber in garments laid away for future use will deteriorate.

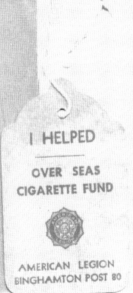

I HELPED

OVER SEAS CIGARETTE FUND

AMERICAN LEGION
BINGHAMTON POST 80

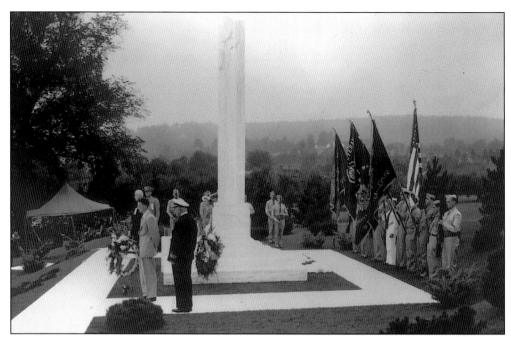

When World War II ended, 57 IBM soldiers lay dead. A solemn dedication was held for a memorial erected near Watson Boulevard on country club property in 1947. The dedication program stated, "Constructed of Imperial Danby Marble, it was the first of its kind to be erected as a memorial to veterans who gave their lives in WWII." Steps to the pillar were inscribed with the Four Freedoms. An eternal gas candle was lit as a constant symbol of honor and sacrifice.

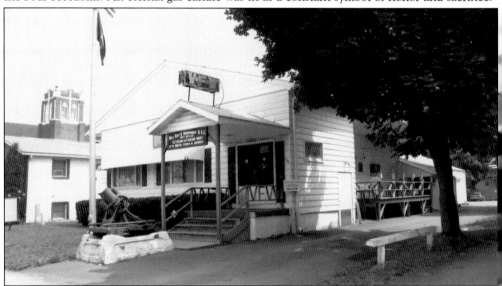

In 1949, with World War II memories fresh, veterans' needs were a community priority. As major corporations in Endicott, IBM and Endicott-Johnson continued assistance to veterans. Two $10,000 checks were presented to the leaders of the Maj. Ray H. Humphrey Post 1449 VFW on Nanticoke Avenue. The funds were used to construct a large addition to its clubhouse. As the VFW boasted a membership of more than 500, the expansion was necessary to provide adequate recreational facilities and an auditorium.

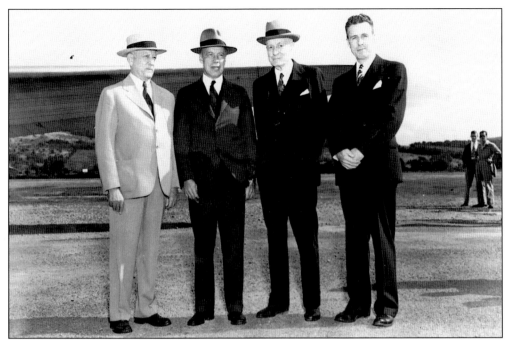

In 1946, Secretary of War Robert Patterson visited Endicott. He complimented IBM president T. J. Watson Sr. on the magnificent machines of the Mobile Machine Records Units in the military. Greeting Secretary Patterson are prominent business leaders. Pictured from left to right are Charles W. Johnson, Robert Patterson, Thomas Watson Sr., and William Paynter.

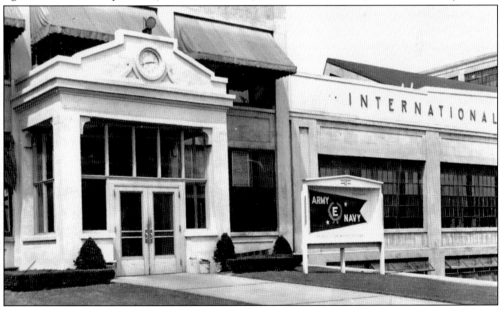

During World War II, IBM had a perfect record for war production. The company never missed a shipping date on any of the 38 major ordinance products and never had an article returned because of poor workmanship. Thus, the Army-Navy "E" for excellence was awarded to IBM for its exemplary participation and superior attendance record. Here, the "E" flag is proudly displayed in front of IBM on North Street.

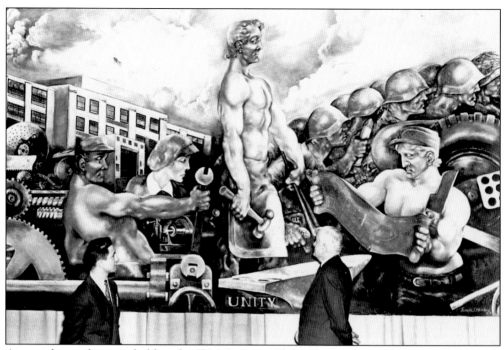

A special unveiling was held at the IBM Country Club's Victory Dawn Dance in 1942. With 1,400 people in attendance, the lights were dimmed in the dining room and a giant mural entitled "Unity" was spotlighted. Dancers were given the honor of being the first to view the painting by Thomas J. Hornby, a member of the bench lathe department. "The painting depicts men and women workers and soldiers blended together in the struggle for the common goal of victory," reported the *Binghamton Press*.

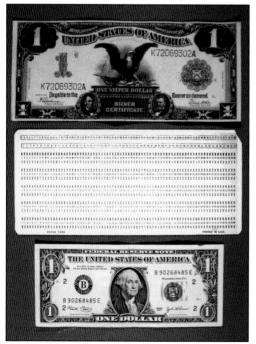

The piece of paperboard that changed world recordkeeping methods—the tabulating card—was originally designed to be the exact size of the old $1 bill (at top). The theory was that people were used to handling currency of this size and would treat the data card (in middle) with the same care as money. Today's dollar is much smaller by comparison.

Four
TENT CITY

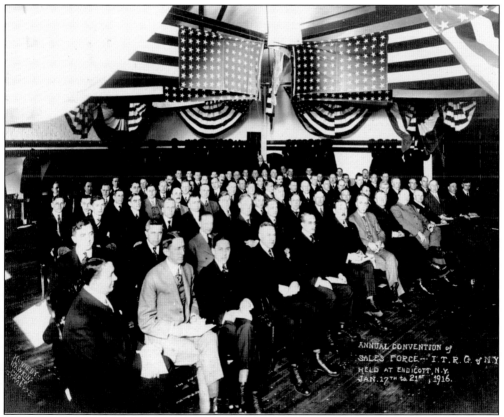

Early in the history of ITR, Watson realized that success depended on key areas in the company: service, sales, and development. To recognize outstanding effort in the sales departments, men who reached and exceeded their sales quotas were invited to a convention in their honor. The One Hundred Percent Club's first meeting was held in Endicott in January 1916 for five days. In that year, the company had a gross income of $4 million and 1,672 employees.

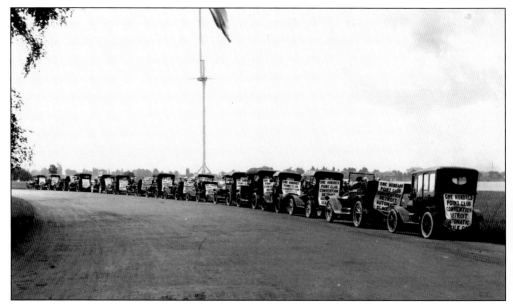

The Hundred Point Club (a forerunner of the One Hundred Percent Club) travels to Detroit in modern vehicles for a 1916 convention. In 1919, it was still a big event when a new automobile arrived in Endicott. A news article reported that an ITR printing department specialist named Bert had joined the ranks of motorists. "He can now be seen via the rubber tire route, aahh, another one to reduce the traction company profits."

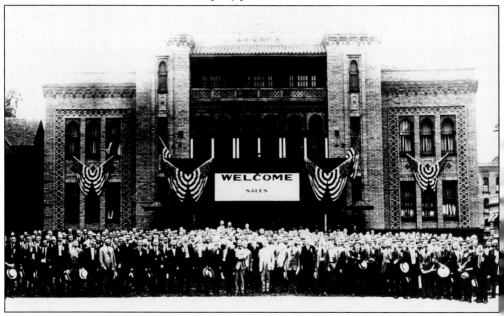

The Arlington Hotel in Binghamton was headquarters for a convention of 300 ITR salesmen in 1919. Sessions and exhibits were held at the Kalurah Temple on Washington Street, pictured above. A feature of the week was a tour and inspection of the Endicott plant. Sales talks, demonstrations of new models and developments, and details of machine workings were discussed. All buildings were lavishly decorated to welcome the largest convention of ITR ever held.

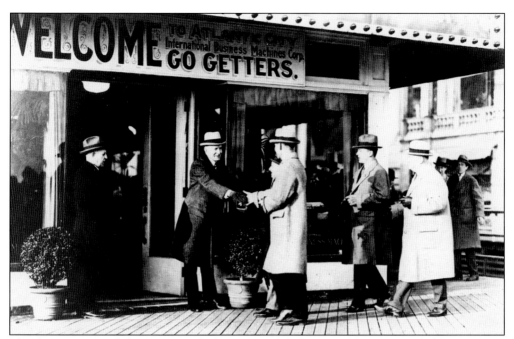

The first meeting of the One Hundred Percent Club for IBM salesmen was held in 1925 in Atlantic City, New Jersey. In this photograph, Watson greets the attendees. His belief was "nothing can happen in a company until somebody sells something." Attendance at this convention was restricted to only the best salesmen, making competition within the sales force intense.

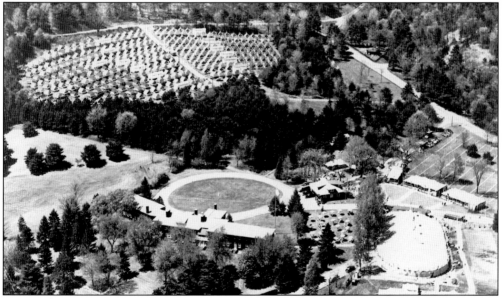

During the 1930s and 1940s, the One Hundred Percent Club met at the IBM Homestead grounds in Endwell. Gigantic corporate pep rallies were held at "Tent City," where 500 two-man tents were erected on the hillsides. A salesman's reward for meeting a sales quota was a week-long stay in a tent. Each attendee was required to have two white shirts available for each day, to always look fresh. IBM's newest product line was displayed, and enthusiasm was generated for future sales.

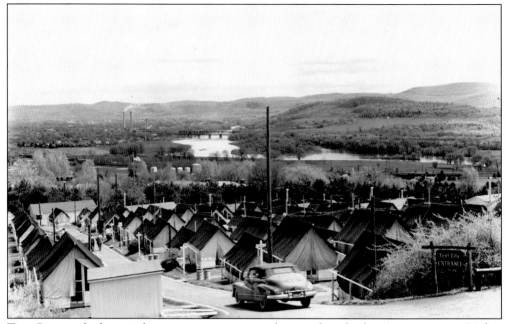

Tent City was laid out with street names, tent numbers, and road rules. A massive tent 38 feet high and 98 feet wide held meetings of 1,000 club members at a time. At the convention, every salesman in attendance was expected to give a speech, and Watson sat through them all, often making notes of evaluation. By the 1950s, the sales convention had outgrown the tent tradition, and thankful members were instead entertained at the Waldorf-Astoria in New York City.

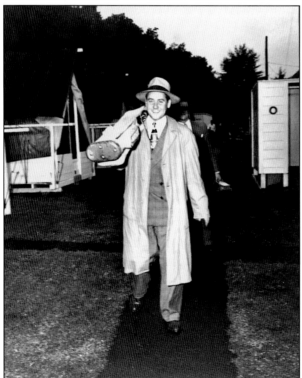

During free time, One Hundred Percent Club members could enjoy the Homestead and country club facilities and attend evening banquets in their honor. First-rate speakers and entertainment were highlights of the meetings. This photograph was taken in 1940.

By 1947, there were 1,500 salesmen en route to the Triple Cities for the largest One Hundred Percent Club meeting in the history of the company. It took four special trains to transport all the attendees to the Binghamton station. IBM financed its own symphony and commissioned an anthem to IBM by Vittorio Giannini. Other odes to Big Blue—such as "Think" (sung to the tune of "Yankee Doodle"), "Ever Onward IBM," and "Hail to Watson"—inspired company loyalty and were printed in an official IBM songbook.

> "EVER ONWARD"
>
> (I. B. M. Rally Song, written especially for the International Business Machines Corporation)
>
> There's a thrill in store for all,
> For we're about to toast
> The corporation that we represent.
> We're here to cheer each pioneer
> And also proudly boast
> Of that "man of men," our sterling president.
> The name of T. J. Watson means a courage none can stem:
> And we feel honored to be here to toast the "I. B. M."
>
> Chorus
>
> EVER ONWARD — EVER ONWARD!
> That's the spirit that has brought us fame!
> We're big, but bigger we will be,
> We can't fail for all can see
> That to serve humanity has been our aim!
> Our products now are known in every zone,
> Our reputation sparkles like a gem!
> We've fought our way through—and new
> Fields we're sure to conquer too
> For the EVER ONWARD I. B. M.
>
> Second Chorus
>
> EVER ONWARD — EVER ONWARD!
> We're bound for the top to never fall!
> Right here and now we thankfully
> Pledge sincerest loyalty
> To the corporation that's the best of all!
> Our leaders we revere, and while we're here
> Let's show the world just what we think of them!
> So let us sing, men! SING, MEN!
> Once or twice then sing again
> For the EVER ONWARD I. B. M.

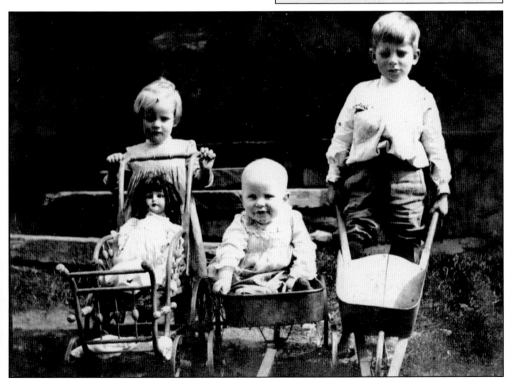

As IBM grew in size and number of locations, all employees were expected to move to whatever site was required of them, especially if they wanted to advance up the corporate ladder. One executive kept this photograph in his office with the unofficial interpretation of the letters IBM printed underneath: "I Been Moved."

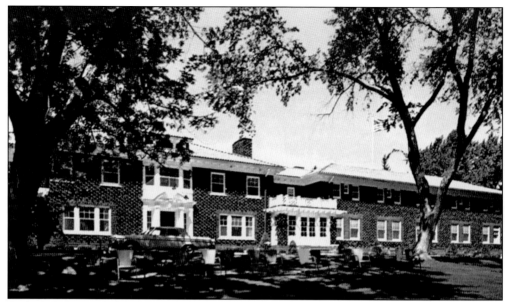

Arthur Gray arrived in Binghamton c. 1808, moved to Union in 1828, and purchased a 350-acre farm. By World War I, the property was owned by Hiram Mintz, who permitted picnicking and allowed the public to cultivate the farmland for war gardens. In 1919, Endicott-Johnson treasurer Elliot Spaulding purchased the parcel and constructed a lavish mansion on the crest of a hillside. The Masonic fraternity then purchased the estate c. 1925 for $100,000, and operated it as the Kalurah Country Club. Due to the Great Depression, foreclosure proceedings made the land available; in the early 1930s, the site was acquired by IBM. The mansion became the Homestead, with wings added for school and dormitory rooms. Watson often stayed at the Homestead, and would give lengthy impromptu talks to "captive" employees and visitors who happened to be in the vicinity. Gen. Dwight D. Eisenhower stayed at the mansion on his visits to the Southern Tier.

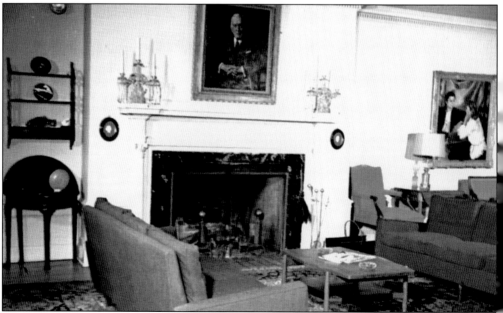

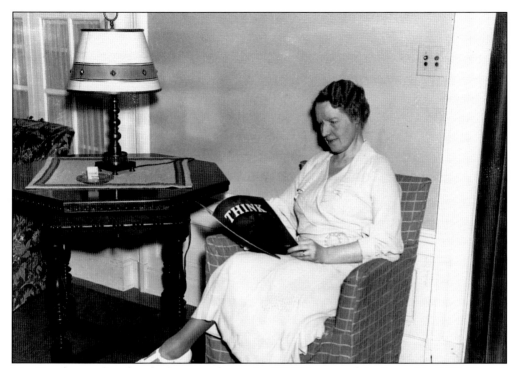

Mrs. Brooks, employed as the housemother at the IBM Homestead, is pictured in 1935. Her job was to maintain the mansion as a clean, efficient, home away from home for Watson, visiting dignitaries, and men attending the IBM schools in Endicott.

When the area of the Homestead land known as Gray's Glen became the IBM Glen in the 1930s, it was enfolded into the country club. A sawmill was set up at the old Gray homestead, and a five-mile roadway was cut through the dense forest. All the cut trees were used as lumber to build structures on the property. A peaceful workers' park was developed for employees. The estate passed from IBM ownership, but not before 205 acres, including the glen, were donated to the community.

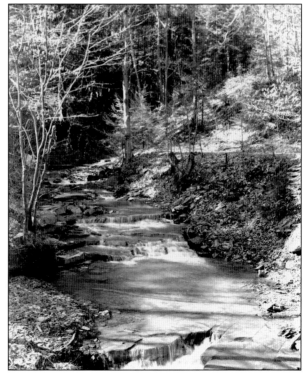

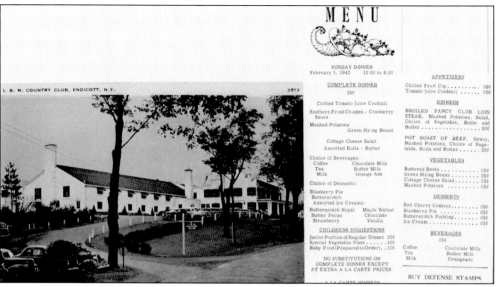

The land and stately brick mansion now part of the IBM Country Club on Watson Boulevard in Endwell was at one time the Crocker family estate. Early in the 1800s, Ezekiel Crocker constructed the building as an inn for stagecoach travelers. The original home burned in 1857, and a similar structure was built on the foundation. IBM purchased the site in 1931, and the 700 acres were turned into a recreation facility. It was considered a symbol of IBM's regard for its employees. Huge wings were added to the building, and a golf course, banquet facilities, gym, tennis courts, pools, bowling alleys, classrooms, and a restaurant were all available at minimal cost to members—just $1 per year. For decades, company retirees were allowed to golf for free on the course pictured below. The IBM restaurant menu is dated 1942.

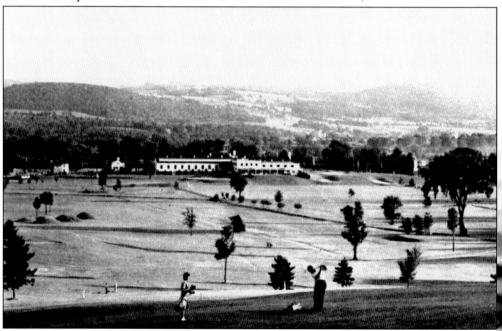

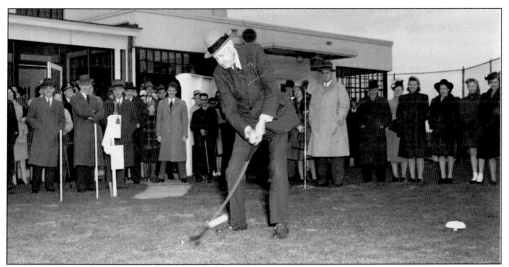

At the grand opening of the golf course at the IBM Country Club in 1940, T. J. Watson Sr. ceremoniously hit the first ball down the fairway. According to company policy, families that worked and played together were good for corporate morale, and "healthy employees are happy employees." The facilities were for the exclusive use of IBM workers, in contrast to Endicott-Johnson, which welcomed the entire community to its parks, pools, cafeterias, and carousels.

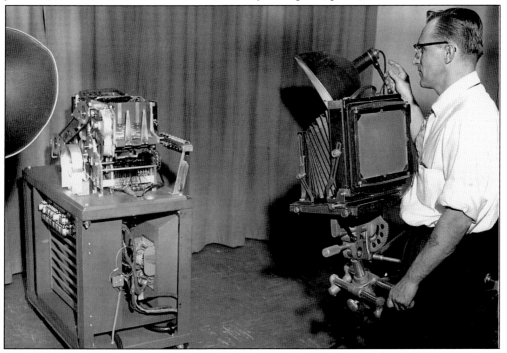

In 1957, the IBM photography lab produced more than 100,000 individual film products. Industrial photography involved all phases of work: educational film strips, advertising, promotion, recruitment, products, and the process of production. IBM also loaned out the services of its photographers for recording community events, paying for all film and processing expenses. Many of the ideas developed in this lab were adopted by major film-producing firms. Seen here is IBM photographer Milt Klish.

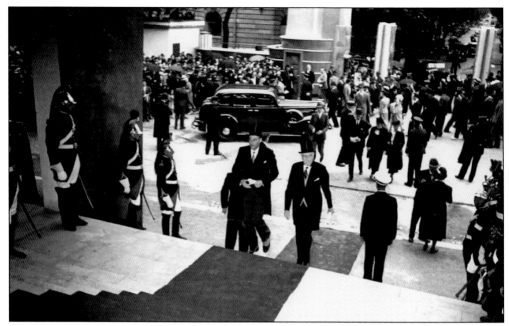

Thomas J. Watson Sr. served as international president of the chamber of commerce in 1937. In this capacity, he traveled more than 70,000 miles throughout the world. He believed peace could be attained through business. The photograph above was taken while Watson was attending a formal meeting in Paris, France.

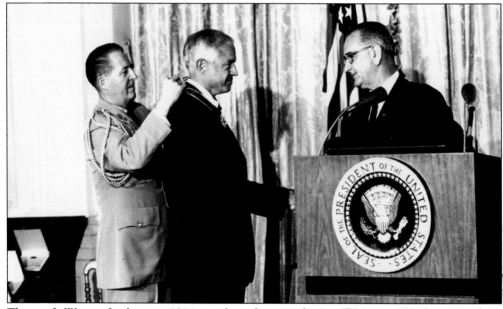

Thomas J. Watson Jr., born in 1914, was brought up to be "an IBM man." He began working at IBM in 1937, staying until the outbreak of World War II. After five years of service as an army pilot, Watson returned to IBM and was elected president in 1952. Under his direction, great strides were made in innovative marketing and providing software and services. These transformations made IBM a world leader in the computer industry. In this 1964 photograph, Watson receives the U.S. Presidential Medal of Freedom from Pres. Lyndon B. Johnson.

Five
IBM Serves Earth and Space

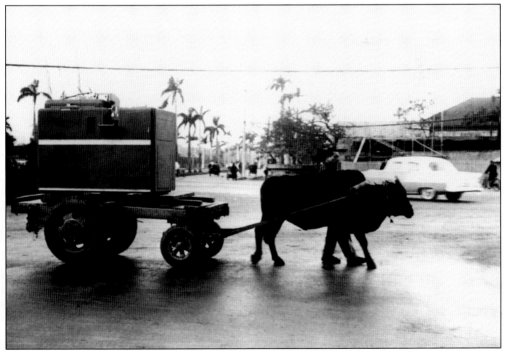

By the late 1950s, IBM business had spread around the world. In 87 foreign countries, 4 laboratories, 22 plants, 262 sales offices, and 29,000 employees served the company. This photograph shows the creative delivery systems used to transport computer components to the headquarters of the Council for the U.S. Aid in Taiwan.

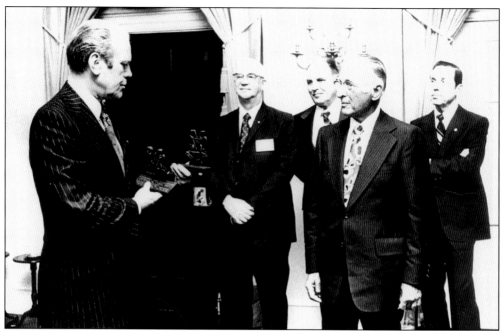

IBM employees were encouraged to participate in community activities. "Service is our duty to society. . . . Service to the community is service to our company. . . . It helps develop real leaders." IBM and its workers were committed to being good "corporate citizens, and to stand for something fine outside a business life." John "Jack" Van Gorden began employment at the company in 1917, combining his work with Masonic duties and philanthropic projects. In 1975, Van Gorden (second from the right) presented Pres. Gerald Ford with a Masonic award.

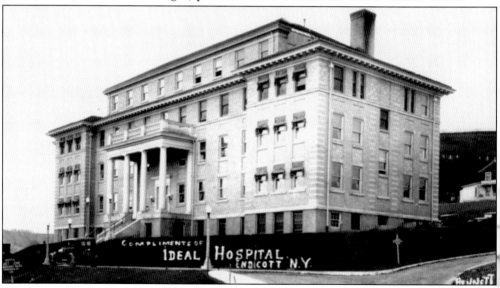

In 1950, Endicott's Ideal Hospital received an entire new parlor in the children's ward, including equipment and beds, courtesy of Endicott IBM personnel and in honor of T. J. Watson Sr. Ideal continued to be a favorite charity, and in 1952, Mrs. T. J. Watson Sr. donated shares of stock and checks for the Ideal furnishing fund totaling more than $41,000. In 1956, she covered most of the cost for a 78-room wing to be added and named in honor of Watson.

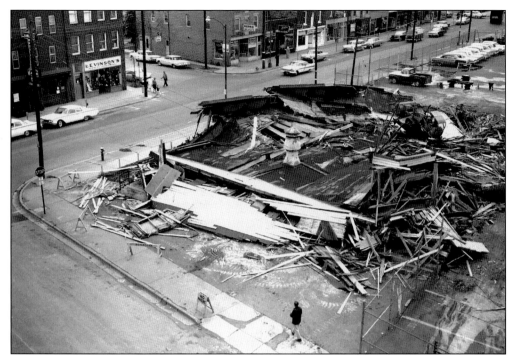

As the days of the great Endicott-Johnson Shoe Corporation began to decline, IBM expanded and replaced aging tannery buildings with modern computer facilities. In 1963, an EJ factory on North Street was demolished (above) to allow for a new building with 180,000 square feet of manufacturing space. The plant was reported to contain equipment and machinery so highly technical, delicate, and expensive that it was the most valuable factory in Broome County when completed.

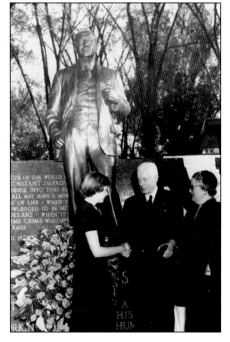

At the unveiling of a public statue to George F. Johnson in 1951, T. J. Watson Sr. (center) joined the Johnson family in praising the memory of a great humanitarian and industrialist. In the early 1900s, Johnson had dissuaded Watson from moving the IBM factories from Endicott. The men remained cordial supporters of the Southern Tier for the rest of their lives.

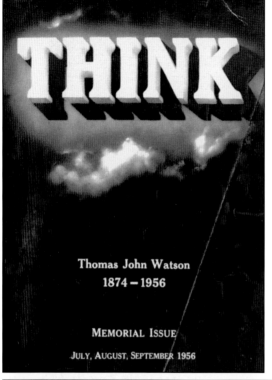

A special memorial issue of *Think* magazine was printed in memory of Thomas John Watson Sr. in 1956. One of the greatest industrialists of the 20th century had died. Watson received many honors and was known for multiple accomplishments; above all, he chose to call himself "a salesman." He was an unofficial ambassador for the United States, believing peace could be maintained by cooperation among businesses of the world. Watson received the highest honor available to a civilian, the Medal of Freedom, bestowed by Pres. Dwight D. Eisenhower. Broome County honored his name by declaring a main thoroughfare Watson Boulevard, and by dedicating a new bridge over the Susquehanna River in his honor in 1963. The bridge is pictured below.

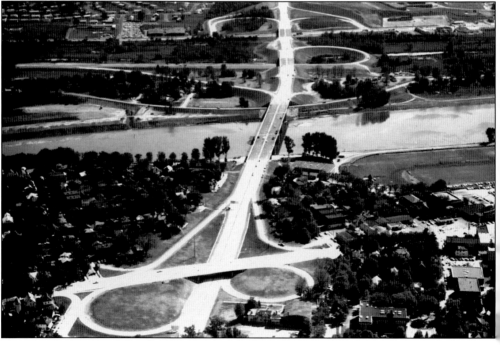

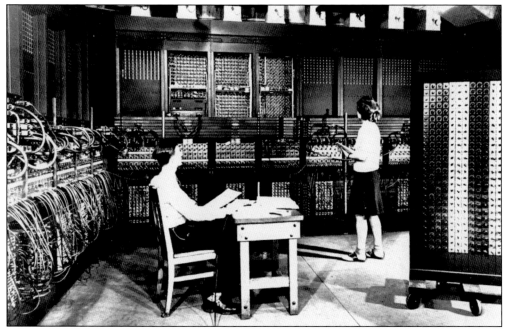

In 1946, the most-modern tabulating technology used miles of wire and had to be housed in a huge room. By 1952, IBM had introduced the first vacuum-tube computer, which could process 17,000 instructions per second. By the 1940s, company policy dictated equal pay for equal work; women at IBM were recognized as valuable employees long before it became the law of the land.

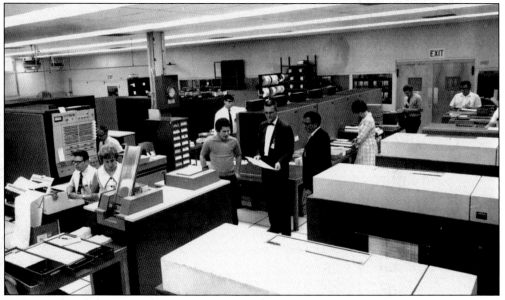

IBM introduced the System/360 in 1964. It was the most important product announcement in the history of the company. This entirely new concept in computers used solid logic technology and stored data on magnetic tape units. System/360 revolutionized the data processing industry, and became one of IBM's most profitable hardware products ever. The number 360 symbolized a circle, or all. Pictured above, the Link Aviation Data Processing Division uses the new computer in 1970. Leonard Robenolt was manager of the department.

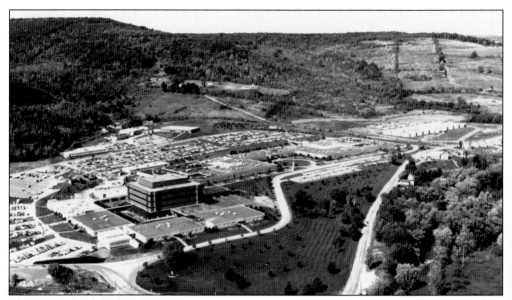

The IBM Glendale development and programming laboratory was built just three and a half miles from the downtown Endicott complex. It began with a 122-acre site and 187,000 square feet of floor space and eventually encompassed 17 buildings. The lobby boasted a wall of Philippine mahogany and birch. The lab's mission was the development of mid-range computer systems, printers, software, applications, and packaged solutions. At its height, more than 17,000 people in the Susquehanna River valley worked for IBM.

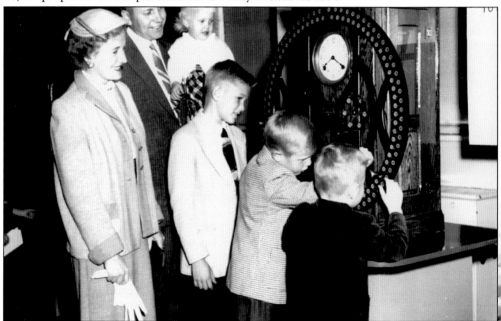

In 1954, an open house was held at the IBM Product Development Laboratory on Glendale Drive in Endicott. Featured there was a grand exhibit of products from 1914 through 1954, as well as products for the future. In this photograph, visitors take advantage of the opportunity to view antique and modern computing and time-recording machines. The attire is typical of the era, including the woman's hat and gloves and the boy's crewcut.

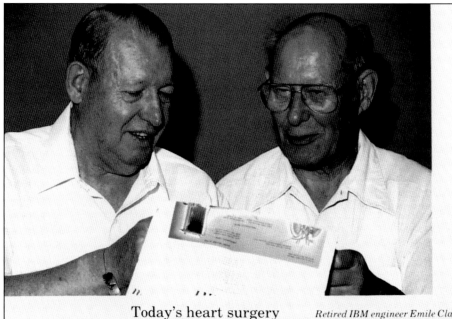

Today's heart surgery miracles made possible by IBM Endicott contributions 40 years ago

Retired IBM engineer Emile Clavez and retired IBM physicist John Engstrom reminisce as they examine old newspaper clippings of the heart-lung machine they helped develop 40 years ago at the Endicott lab.

Many products developed in part or whole by IBM research teams never received a great deal of public notice. Among these products were the artificial arm, the blood separator, and the heart-lung machine. The mechanical heart-lung apparatus was developed in 1953. It was the first machine that could function as both heart and lungs for a human patient during surgery. Pictured above are two of the scientists involved in the project, and at right, a letter from Thomas J. Watson Jr. commending the men on their achievement.

THOMAS J. WATSON, JR.
590 MADISON AVENUE
NEW YORK 22, N.Y.

July 20, 1953

Dear Mr. Engstrom,

    Dr. Gibbon, of the Jefferson Medical College, has had a great deal of success with the artificial heart and lung which IBM helped to develop.

    As you know, we decided that there would be no publicity in connection with IBM's part in this program, but I would like to take this opportunity to express our appreciation for the important part you played in this project, making it possible for this company to make a real contribution to medical science.

    With all good wishes,

Sincerely yours,

Tom Watson Jr

Mr. John R. Engstrom
International Business Machines Corporation
Endicott, New York

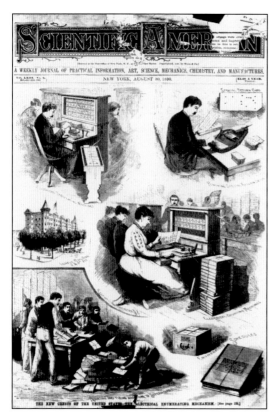

Data storage progressed from the great innovation of punched cards to magnetic tape in less than a century. The punch card process was hailed on the cover of *Scientific American* in 1890, as shown in the photograph at left. The magnetic tape revolution and the huge storage cabinets for the reels are depicted below. At the top is a composite of photographs of the modern "tape data storage system" at the Glendale laboratory; at the bottom is a sample of the tape with an explanation of magnetic tape storage printed on the ever-present tabulating card.

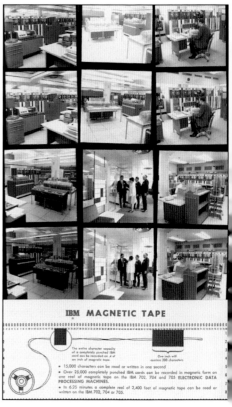

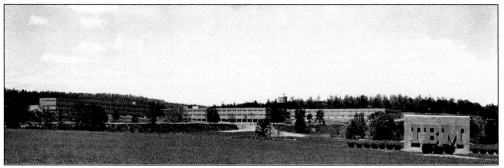

IBM built a modern fortress to house the Military Products and the Federal Systems Divisions 10 miles west of Endicott. Just outside Owego, on 885 acres, a huge campus consisting of 566,000 square feet of working space was in operation. Thousands of people were employed in the massive structure. The U.S. Space Program depended heavily on the computers, tracking systems, and guidance programs developed at this site. The campus is shown above, and a collage of space-age developments appears below. The small acrylic bubble was an early space computer the size of a bowling ball. The room-size device was a prototype of the Saturn rocket instrument unit. The cold room was used for testing components under frigid conditions. IBM was a major contributor of technology that made space exploration possible.

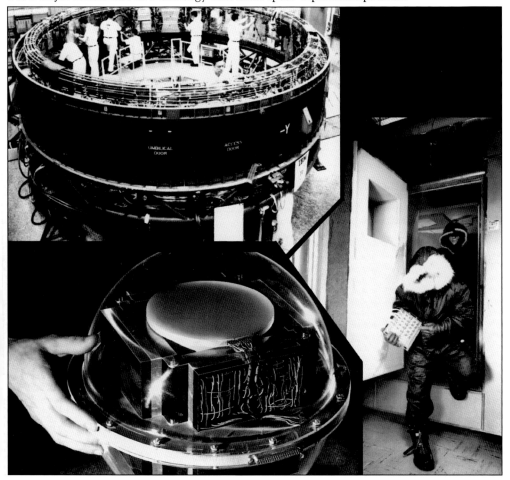

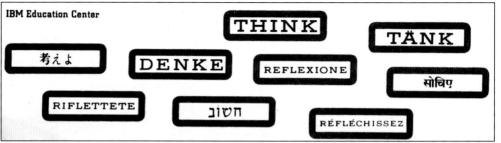

The most famous corporate motto in history was coined by T. J. Watson Sr. when he worked for the National Cash Register Company. "Think" was considered a Watson masterpiece—a mantra, slogan, and way of life for employees. Here, it is translated into multiple languages, though in IBM locations all over the world, the language of business was English.

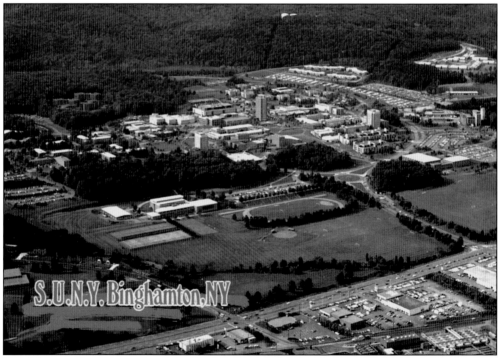

The Thomas J. Watson Sr. School of Engineering and Applied Science at Binghamton University was dedicated in 1984. IBM pledged $50,000 a year for five years to begin the school. Watson took the local slogan "Valley of Opportunity" to heart, believing technology was the future of IBM and the local economy. The Watson School continues to provide engineers and computer scientists with an exceptional education.

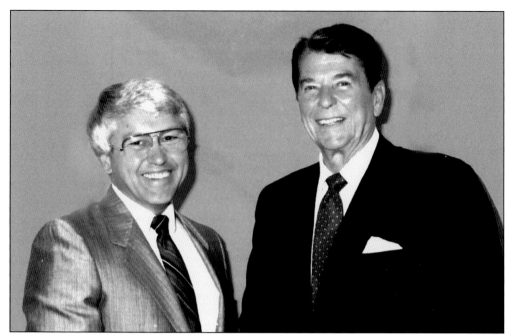

In September 1984, the IBM Endicott facility was host to a visit from Pres. Ronald Reagan. The president toured the plant, viewed exhibits of the history of computing equipment, and gave a speech to thousands of residents at the Union-Endicott High School stadium. Above, IBM Systems Technology Division president P. A. Toole poses with Reagan. Below, the president stands at the podium at Ty Cobb Stadium. (Photographs by Ed Aswad.)

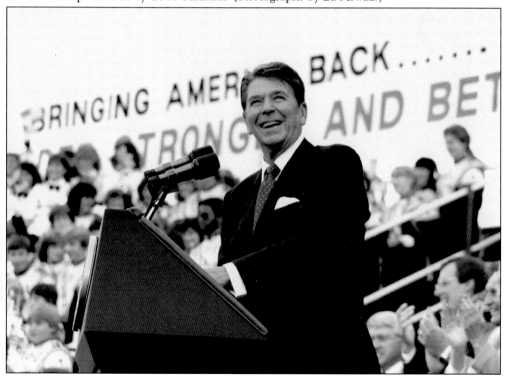

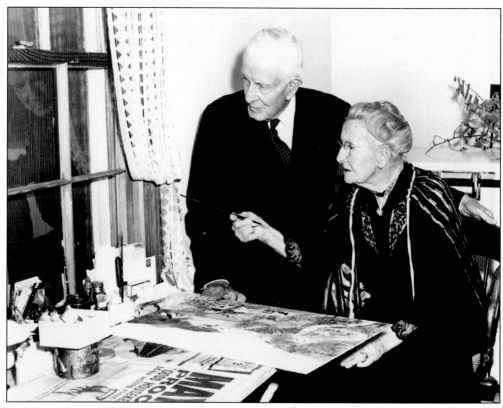

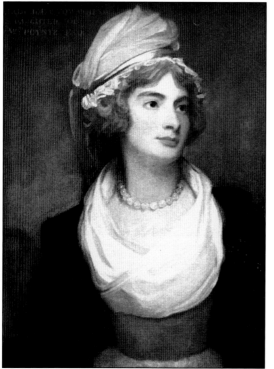

The extensive corporate art collection belonging to IBM was begun by Watson during preparations for the 1939 World's Fair. His personal interest in art was so great that Pres. Franklin D. Roosevelt appointed him to chair the second National Week of Art. IBM owned paintings, sculpture, and an array of small-scale working models of Leonardo da Vinci's inventions. Watson encouraged a close relationship between business and art and made exhibits of great art available to the public. Watson was also one of the first to bring attention to the primitive artist Grandma Moses, whom he is pictured with above. *Lady Townshend*, the painting at left, was created by English artist George Romney and was part of the IBM Institutional Collection.

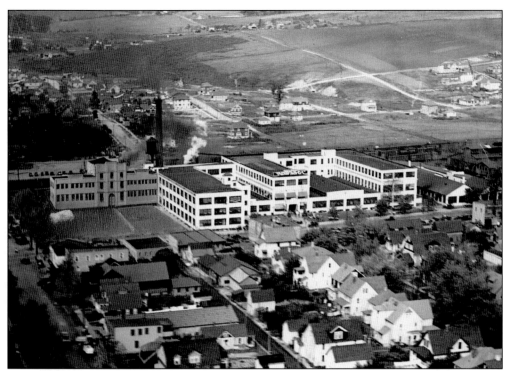

The tremendous impact IBM had on the village of Endicott and all of Broome County is symbolized by these photographs. The picture above was taken in 1920, when there were only 2,731 employees at CTR. The photograph below was taken by Ed Aswad in 1990, when the economy and every aspect of the local scene was dominated by the presence of the paternalistic computer giant. The entire complex of IBM buildings has since been sold and a small area has been rented for the fewer than 1,700 remaining IBM employees in Endicott. Images carved in stone on several of the older structures endure—including symbols of computing roots, a stylized abacus, an hourglass, and scales—but IBM has left the buildings . . . and the birthplace of computing technology.

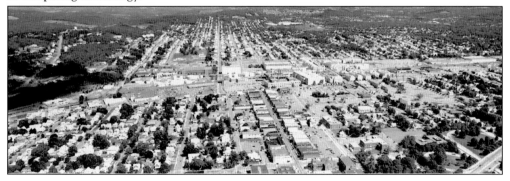

ACKNOWLEDGMENTS

We are grateful to the following individuals and organizations for their assistance with this book:

The Town of Union History Center
  at the Amos Patterson Museum
Denny Cartner
Harold Cole
William Davies
David J. Desimone
John Eingstrom
Robert Gongleski
Milt Klish
Bob Novak

Leonard Robenolt
Robert Strubble
Rudolph Sutherland
Patty Tebeek
Tuthils' Photo
Laddie Vana
Douglas Wagner
Wegman's Photo Department
Jack White

    Special thanks are due to the following: the IBM Corporate Archives in Somers, New York; its manager, Paul Lasewicz; reference archivist Dawn Stanford, the gracious lady who coordinated visits and archive access; associate archivist Stacy Fortner, who did all the scanning of the old photographs; associate archivist Jennifer Holleran; and Ken Sayers, IBM Archives Web site editor.
    The entire project would not have been possible without the unqualified support and advice from Todd L. Martin of IBM Communications.

BIBLIOGRAPHY

Belden, Thomas and Marva. *The Lengthening Shadow*. Boston: Little, Brown & Co., 1962.
IBM Corporation. *As a Man Thinks*. 1954. Selected writings by Thomas J. Watson Sr. published by IBM in recognition of Watson's 40th-anniversary year at IBM.
———. *IBM: Dedicated to Progress*. 1948.
———. *Dedicated to Victory*. 1942. A historical record of War Rally Parade.
———. *IBM Heritage Calendar*. 1988.
———. *Think* magazine. Multiple issues from 1938 to 1990.
———. *Think* magazine. "Diary of U.S. Participation in World War II." 1950.
———. *Think* magazine. Special bicentennial issue. July 1976.
———. *Think* magazine. 75th anniversary edition.
———. *WW II Memorial Dedication*. 1947.
IBM One Hundred Percent Club. *Yearbook*. 1949.
IBM Quarter Century Club. *The First Half Century of the Quarter Century Club*.
International Time Recording Company. *Mechanical and Electrical Service Manual*. 1926.
McIntire, Stephen. *Harpur College in the Bartle Era*. Binghamton, NY: Foundation of the State University of New York, 1975.